Surgeons' Halls

*Royal College of Surgeons in Ireland, St Stephen's Green.
Engraved from a drawing by George Petrie, 1821.*

*St Stephen's Green West: 1750 (top), 1810 and 1830.
Drawing by Stephen Conlin.*

Surgeons' Halls

Building the Royal College of
Surgeons in Ireland 1810–2010

Edited by Clive Lee

Foreword by
Frank Keane,
President of RCSI
2008–2010

Royal College of Surgeons in Ireland
in association with
A. & A. Farmar

© Texts: the contributors 2011
© Editorial selection and assembly: the Royal College of Surgeons
in Ireland 2011

Design layout and typesetting by Bookworks
Cover design by A. & A. Farmar
Printed and bound by ColourBooks

All rights reserved. No part of this publication may be reproduced in any
form or by any means without the prior permission of the publisher or else
under the terms of a licence permitting photocopying issued by the Irish
Copyright Licensing Agency or a similar reproductive rights organisation.

British Library Cataloguing in Publication Data
A CIP catalogue record for this book is available from the British Library

ISBN: 978-1-906353-22-3

First published in 2011 by
A. & A. Farmar Ltd
78 Ranelagh Village, Dublin 6, Ireland
Tel +353-1-496 3625 Fax +353-1-497 0107
Email: afarmar@iol.ie Web: aafarmar.ie
in association with
Royal College of Surgeons in Ireland

The publishers thank the institutions and individuals who have kindly
provided photographic materials for use in this book. In all cases, every effort
has been made to contact the copyright holders, but should there be any
errors or omissions, the publishers would be pleased to insert the appropriate
acknowledgement in any subsequent edition of this book.

Front cover: Anonymous, Royal College of Surgeons 1810, watercolour
Back cover: Royal College of Surgeons in Ireland–Medical University of Bahrain
viewed from the northwest.
Drawing of St Stephen's Green from Dublin: One Thousand Years *by*
Stephen Conlin, published by The O'Brien Press Ltd, Dublin, 1988,
Copyright © Stephen Conlin

Contents

Foreword *Frank B. V. Keane* — vii

A history of the Royal College of Surgeons in Ireland — 1
Clive Lee & Mary O'Doherty

'Simply elegant'—the original building of — 15
the Royal College of Surgeons in Ireland
Patricia McCarthy

The College buildings in context — 69
Christopher Moore

The 2010 Widdess Lecture: — 96
Corridic modernities—space and interiority
in nineteenth- & twentieth-century architecture
Mark Jarzombek

Royal College of Surgeons in Ireland-
Medical University of Bahrain, 2009 — 153
Colin Stewart

Contributors

Mark Jarzombek is Professor of the History and Theory of Architecture at Massachusetts Institute of Technology and RCSI Widdess Lecturer, 2010.

Clive Lee is Professor of Anatomy in the Royal College of Surgeons in Ireland.

Patricia McCarthy is an architectural historian.

Christopher Moore is an architectural historian.

Mary O'Doherty is Assistant Librarian, Special Collections and Archives, in the Royal College of Surgeons in Ireland.

Colin Stewart is Associate Director of Estate and Support Services in the Royal College of Surgeons in Ireland.

Acknowledgements

The support of the 2010 Committee is gratefully acknowledged: Frank McManus (Chair), Niamh Burdett, Jennifer Cullinane, Joe Duignan, Tom Gorey, Frank Keane, Parnell Keeling, Clive Lee, Louise Loughran, Eilis McGovern, Terry McWade, Caroline Murphy, Margaret Nolan, Mary O'Doherty and Colin Stewart

Foreword

I am delighted to have been asked to write a foreword to this compilation of fine essays that have been commissioned to commemorate the 200th anniversary of the first building of the Royal College of Surgeons on St Stephen's Green in 1810.

During my presidency one of the journeys that I made took me to India and to the city of Hyderabad. Outside Hyderabad are the remains of a fortress citadel, named Golconda. It was once famous for its diamond trade and, according to legend, everyone who passed through became rich. Another interesting feature about it was that amongst its splendid monuments there is a perfect acoustic system such that, if one claps ones hands at the fort's main gates, the sound can be heard at the citadel placed on a hill some distance away.

This struck me as an interesting metaphor for RCSI on two counts. Firstly, it is both our understanding and hope that everyone who passes through its corridors becomes rich, not merely in material gain, but in knowledge, companionship, disposition and confidence. The second part of the metaphor reflects this College's ability to reverberate its message great distances, indeed to the many corners of the globe.

The grandeurs of Golconda have long since faded, reminding us that buildings are merely bricks and mortar and are often forgotten in the day to day activities of institutions which, in truth, are born of ideas and draw their inspiration from the men and women who work in them. But their presence does offer a comfortable feeling of aesthetic satisfaction and solidity, as well as providing a time-line to the past. It is in that sense that this book recognises their value and ability to survive despite the turbulence of history. What has resulted is a celebration for the reader of the College buildings, both old and new, together with an absorbing journey through their interwoven stories.

The book opens with a brief but lively account of the College's history put together by Clive Lee and Mary O'Doherty, each in their own particular way possessors of a deep knowledge repository of our College's past.

Patricia McCarthy's essay brings us back to 1784 when the St Stephen's Green building was first conceived and then takes us from the purchase of the site through its planning, construction and subsequent rebuilding

FOREWORD

to what we see today. She describes in great detail the personalities involved as well as the structures themselves and the provenance of the ideas that shaped them.

The next essay is written by Christopher Moore and, as its title suggests, it places the buildings in context. There is a curious symmetry to the fact that the College was built at a time of financial depression, much as we find ourselves in in 2010. At a time when the aristocratic ascendancy was being replaced by the professional classes, so architecture drifted in its various fashions during the Regency period. We also hear, in this chapter, about the College art collection and a brief account of later building developments.

Professor Jack Widdess served RCSI for many years and in many guises and was ultimately Professor of Biology. The Widdess Lecture was instituted in his memory and we had the privilege of hearing this year's eponymous lecture given by Mark Jarzombek, a distinguished architectural historian. The text of this lecture is the fourth essay and entitled, 'Corridic modernities—space and interiority in 19th and 20th Century Architecture'. This academic treatise takes us much further into a grander scale of architecture that was developing in Europe at the same time as the College was being built and brings us right through to the present time; and all from the singular perspective of 'the corridor'.

Lastly, but very much not least, is the essay by Colin Stewart who describes both the concept and construction of the iconic RCSI Medical University building in Bahrain which was completed and opened by the President of Ireland, Mary McAleese, in 2009. It draws a sharp contrast between the building methods, designs and practices of the twenty-first century and those of the early nineteenth century, but also between their incomparably different situations.

We are greatly indebted to all the authors for their magnificent contributions. The work of Clive Lee has to be especially acknowledged as not only being the inspiration behind the book, but also for his many ideas and concepts right up to its publication. We owe our publishers a debt of gratitude for the fine presentation and the rich display of illustrations.

In the end this volume is a testament to where we are now and where we have come from. It is also, I am sure, a wonderful point of departure as we begin to create the history of the next two hundred years.

Professor Frank B. V. Keane, *President 2008–2010*

A history of the Royal College of Surgeons in Ireland

Clive Lee & Mary O'Doherty

Origins

The Dublin Society of Surgeons was founded in 1780. According to Sir Philip Crampton, Surgeon-General to the Lord Lieutenant and four times President of the College, at this time Irish surgery was

> immeasurably below medicine in everything which could ground a claim to public confidence and respect. In one word, with a few, and *there were very few*, exceptions, the surgeons were at this period uneducated men, few of them had a university education, none of them had a clinical education.[1]

Fifty years later, however, an editorial in the *Edinburgh Medical Journal* described the Royal College of Surgeons in Dublin as 'perhaps the most enlightened surgical corporation in Europe' which required of its members 'a greater range of accurate knowledge than any other body, excepting the Medical Faculty of the University of Edinburgh.'[2] This *caveat* notwithstanding, enormous progress had been made in little over half a century by the Royal College of Surgeons in Ireland.

The Dublin Society of Surgeons met for the first time under the Presidency of Henry Morris, surgeon to Mercer's Hospital, in The Elephant in Essex Street, a public house named after an animal on exhibition which had perished in a fire on the site in 1681. Meetings were held on Thursdays, a tradition which still endures, and in June the Society resolved that

> a Royal Charter, dissolving the preposterous and disgraceful union of the surgeons of Dublin with the barbers, and incorporating them separately and distinctly, upon liberal and scientific principles, would highly contribute, not only to their own emolument and the advancement of the profession in Ireland, but to the good of society in general by cultivating and diffusing surgical knowledge.[3]

Royal Charter

A formal petition was presented to the Lord Lieutenant in 1781 and, despite objections from the Barber-Surgeons Guild, a charter was granted by George III on 11 February 1784, supporting the foundation of a College to regulate the practice of surgery and to make provision for surgical education. The Royal College of Surgeons in Ireland met for the first time in the Board Room of the Rotunda Hospital on 2 March 1784. Samuel Croker-King, the College's first President, was a veteran of two unsuccessful petitions for a charter in the 1770s.

In November 1785, John Halahan was appointed Professor of Anatomy and Physiology and William Dease, Professor of Surgery. The professors were paid according to the numbers of students who attended their lectures. They received three guineas for each 'stranger' and two guineas from each registered pupil of the College and gave the courses on their own premises, as well as conducting their own private practices.

Mercer Street

From 1785, the College regularly petitioned Parliament for money to build a hall but without success for 'though government highly approved of their institution . . . it was highly impossible in the present state of the country's finances to allow any aid in money.'[4] Then, as since, the College decided to exercise its independence and leased premises in Mercer Street which had formerly been occupied by the charity children of the local parish of St Peter's. Rent was fixed at £26 per annum, over one-third of the College's income. The two professors therefore needed no more than twelve students to earn as much as the College was paying in rent.

These premises were dilapidated and required extensive refurbishment at a cost of over £500. An adjacent house was bought for £100 in order to gain access to Goat Alley, now Digges Lane, through which the resurrectionists might secretly bring bodies for the dissecting room. The Schools of the College were thus ready for occupation by October 1789, just as the French Revolution broke out in Paris. The ever-increasing demand for surgeons caused by the Anglo-French wars over the next twenty-five years was to be a major factor in the development of the College. Classes began with Halahan and William Hartigan as joint

Professors of Anatomy and Physiology. Halahan held also the first Chair of Midwifery in Ireland. The newly-established Chair of Surgical Pharmacy was filled by Clement Archer.

The first chair devoted to surgery in these islands was occupied by William Dease. President of the College in 1789, he was connected to the United Irishmen, a secret society dedicated to securing independence from England. When warned during the 1798 Rebellion by George Stewart, the Surgeon-General, that his arrest was imminent, Dease 'went home from the College…opened the femoral artery and died of haemorrhage.'[5] His statue in the College entrance hall is by Thomas Farrell RHA, and, appropriately, a crack in the marble of the left thigh follows the course of the superficial femoral artery.

In 1785, the Lord Lieutenant had requested that the College examine candidates for the offices of surgeon and surgeon's mate with the result that, for many years, the Court of Examiners had more candidates for these certificates than for the Letters Testimonial of the College. The oldest surviving student records are for 1792 when a hundred attended, including army surgeons. Demand for army and navy surgeons increased from 1793 with the declaration of war with France. The Government proved not ungrateful for the College's efforts.

Abraham Colles

In 1790, Abraham Colles, a seventeen-year-old student from Kilkenny registered as a pupil in the College. Colles was also reading Arts at the University and was apprenticed to Philip Woodroffe, surgeon to Dr Steevens' Hospital. He attended anatomy and physiology lectures given by Halahan and Hartigan and the latter's syllabus, published in 1796, outlines a course of 103 lectures given between November and April. The course was taught system by system, beginning with osteology, then myology, angiology, neurology, respiration, digestion, secretion and the urinary organs, and finally generation. To Colles, this approach was like attempting to

> explain the mechanism of a watch, by taking it to pieces, and giving a separate description of every particular wheel and spring without afterwards attempting to show by what contrivance the one moves the other . . . the student who has

been shown the venous, arterial and nervous systems of the arm, does not know how each of them lies with respect to each other.[6]

Colles received his Letters Testimonial of the RCSI in 1795, was elected a Member in 1799, President in 1802 and Professor of Anatomy and Physiology and Professor of Surgery in 1804. He revolutionised teaching in the College by approaching anatomy topographically, rather than systematically, seeking 'to describe the relative position of the parts, and to point out the subservience of anatomical knowledge to surgical practice.'[7] His book describing this approach, *A Treatise on Surgical Anatomy*, was dedicated to the President, Members and Licentiates of the Royal College of Surgeons in Ireland. In it, Colles described the ligament and fascia which bear his name. His original description of the fracture of the distal radius was later published in the *Edinburgh Medical and Surgical Journal* in 1814. A contemporary of Colles at the College School was James Macartney, who subsequently became Professor of Anatomy and Chirurgery in Trinity College in 1813 and revived its then flagging medical school.

St Stephen's Green

'Surgeons', by contrast, was booming. By 1804 larger premises were required, Parliament was petitioned, and the Government, seeing the advantage of supporting a body whose school supplied so many competent army and navy surgeons, granted £6,000. George Renny purchased the former Quaker burial ground fronting onto St Stephen's Green, building started in 1806 and the new surgeons' hall was completed in 1810. The construction of this three-bay Roman temple, its expansion to seven bays in the 1820s and remodelling in the 1870s are described by Patricia McCarthy in the second chapter of this book 'Simply elegant— the original building of the Royal College of Surgeons in Ireland'.

At its foundation in 1784, the College resolved to establish a library, levying one guinea annually from members. Three decades later this received a boost when on its dissolution, the Physico-Chirurgical Society (1790–1816) sold its books to the College. The antiquarian collections comprise early printed books, special collections, pamphlets, archives, manuscripts, drawings, news cuttings and photographs. The early printings represent the history of medicine and surgery, while the

extensive collections of pamphlets, manuscripts and archi
foreign and local historical developments. The great Euro
houses are represented—the earliest printings date from
extraordinary plate books and most of the advances in me
or early editions are held. Natural history, travel, literature
ties formed a considerable part of the collection.

By 1819, the College had resolved 'that it is highly expedient to establish a Museum to contain specimens of natural history and such other
sciences as are subservient to surgery.'[8] Its first Curator, John Shekleton,
suffered the fate of many early anatomists. Colles, who was present on
that fatal day, Tuesday 18 May 1824, wrote:

> engaged in examining the body of a man who had died of peritoneal inflamma-
> tion . . . Mr Shekleton pricked himself with the point of his knife, which called
> forth the usual involuntary expression of pain, but was not further attended
> to. He proceeded to take out the contents of the pelvis, so that his hands were
> necessarily immersed in that cavity for a considerable time.[9]

Shekleton fell ill on the following day and died of sepsis nine days
later. John Houston, Shekleton's assistant, succeeded him as Curator.
Eponymously known for his description of the valves of the rectum,
Houston noted that the mucosa was 'made uneven in several places by
certain valvular projections . . . three is the average number . . . the form
of the valves is semilunar.'[10] It was Houston also who was responsible
for assembling the Northumberland Wax Collection of the College,
following a donation from the Lord Lieutenant 'as a lasting testament
to his approbation and esteem.'[11] This collection comprises the largest
surviving body of works by the celebrated French artist Jacques Talrich.[12]
The only other recorded extant piece is the head of Jeremy Bentham in
University College, London—for which Talrich is better known.[13] The
anatomical detail and accuracy and the lustrous colouration of Talrich's
models are remarkable, but interest in waxes declined due to the increased
availability of cadavers following the Anatomy Act of 1832.

A College of medicine and surgery

At the request of the British Army Board, a Chair of Medicine was
created in 1813 to which John Cheyne, a Scotsman and prolific medical
author who had not long begun to practice in Dublin, was appointed. He

lectured chiefly on military surgery and medicine. He was a co-founder of the *Dublin Hospital Reports,* one of the earliest medical journals published in Ireland. In its second volume in 1818, Cheyne published his eponymous account of terminal breathing:

> it would utterly cease for a quarter of a minute, then it would become perceptible, though very low, then by degrees it became heavy and quick, and then it would gradually cease again.[14]

Cheyne was succeeded by Whitley Stokes, whose son William, the Stokes of Cheyne-Stokes Respiration, was a pupil in the College School and subsequently Professor of Physic at Trinity College Dublin. Arthur Jacob was appointed to the Chair of Anatomy and Physiology on Colles's resignation in 1827. He had attended the College School and worked under Macartney in Trinity where he was the first in 1819 to describe the layer of rods and cones in the retina—Jacob's Membrane.[15] He held most of the major offices of the College and was twice President—in 1837 and 1864. Sir Charles Cameron, the College historian, describes Jacob as the College School's 'uncompromising champion'.[16] In 1844, Jacob addressed the new students:

> This College, although called a College of Surgeons, is, as you all know, just as much a College of Physicians. We have the same corps of professors, or even a larger one; we require the same course of medical studies, or even a more extended one; and we examine as carefully on medical subjects as they do in the schools of medicine. In fact, this is a College of Medicine and Surgery, and the Diploma you receive from it is universally accepted as evidence of your fitness to practice every branch of the healing art.[17]

In 1999, the late J. B. Lyons expanded on this theme in his book *A Pride of Professors: The Professors of Medicine at the Royal College of Surgeons in Ireland 1813–1985.*[18]

Private schools of medicine

The continuing demand for medical personnel for the army and navy meant that the College school was not alone in flourishing. From 1804 onwards seventeen private medical schools were founded, named after hospitals, such as the Jervis Street School, or prominent medical teachers, such as the Carmichael. The majority of students, however, came to the College of Surgeons for their formal qualification. As a result, the teaching in these schools came under the control of the College since their survival depended on their courses being recognised by RCSI.[19] By the 1880s the requirements for practical teaching were making such schools uneconomical so that in 1888, the Fellows resolved that

> having regard to the interests of medical education in Dublin, it is desirable to diminish, as far as possible, the number of private schools; and that, with a view to carrying out this principle, it be an earnest recommendation to the Council to take such steps as may be necessary to effect on equitable terms, an amalgamation of the existing private schools with the School of the College of Surgeons.[20]

Eventually amalgamation took place, with the new entity being styled 'The Schools of Surgery of the Royal College of Surgeons in Ireland, including the Carmichael and Ledwich Schools.' The College acquired the Carmichael premises, while those of the Ledwich were bought by the Adelaide Hospital.

Licence and degree

The Medical Act of 1858 turned medicine into a regulated profession by establishing the Register of the General Medical Council. Hereafter applicants for any public medical post, whether in the forces or in the poor law, had to be on the Register. The Act formally recognised the College's Licentiate as one of the qualifications. The change gave rise to a long-running series of negotiations between the College and the College of Physicians. The amendment of 1886 requiring the triple qualification in medicine, surgery and midwifery concentrated the minds of both institutions. They agreed on a 'scheme for constituting an Examining Board in Ireland by the King and Queen's College of Physicians of Ireland and the Royal College of Surgeons in Ireland'.[21]

Despite a brief liaison with the Apothecaries' Hall from 1887 to 1894, the union with the RCPI has continued to this day. It has not, of course, been without incident. Shortly after the first joint conferring, the College of Physicians informed the surgeons that their bye-laws required that their diploma be always conferred in *their* Hall. The College responded in kind, resolving that their diploma must be conferred in the College of Surgeons. For 85 years therefore, the graduates were conferred LRCSI in the College in the morning, solemnly repairing to Kildare Street after

[7]

lunch to become LRCPI.[22] By 1973, common sense had prevailed.

Academic standards were rising by then, and in the mid 1970s it was recognised that 'the surgeons graduate, through no fault of his own, due to his inability to proceed to MD or MS degrees may find himself at a considerable disadvantage in competing for positions'.[23] Negotiations were entered into with both the National University of Ireland and the University of Dublin. An agreement was reached in 1977 whereby the College would become a recognised college of the National University of Ireland, with its licentiates receiving the degrees MB, BCh, BAO.[24] History had come full circle: in 1858 the College had helped to ensure the success of the Catholic University Medical School by recognising its lectures in Cecilia Street.

Easter, 1916

On Easter Monday 1916, a Fellow of the College, John Knott, arrived to study in the Library of the College. The porter opened the door to tell him that the College had been closed by order of the Registrar, but before he could shut it, Countess Markievicz and two Citizen Army men entered the College at gunpoint. Over the following week, over a hundred men, women and boys occupied the College and barricaded the Front Hall with books from the Library, slept in the College Hall, used the space beneath the seats of the Chemistry Lecture Theatre as a mortuary and the Anatomy Lecture Theatre for community singing of patriotic songs.[25] Shooting from outside was concentrated on the Board Room overlooking St Stephen's Green, with the Tuscan columns of the façade, the Colles portrait and the copper finger plate of the door leading to the stairs all receiving bullet damage. Following Pearse's order to lay down arms on Saturday, the College garrison surrendered on Sunday, 30 April. The events of Easter Week are commemorated by a plaque on the façade of the College, at the corner of St Stephen's Green and Glover's Alley.

The new College

By the 1960s the College faced the same dilemma as had the private schools in the 1880s—scientific advances demanded new and costly facilities for teaching and research. The Registrar, Dr Harry O'Flanagan,

[8]

summarised the situation when he joined RCSI in 1962:

> the total income of the College was £66,500. The Council owned the College, the Schools in York Street and the five adjacent houses. The Bird Avenue playing fields were leased. There were ten Professorships, of these three were in the basic sciences, and whole-time. The Medical School required to be re-equipped with instruments and teaching aids. There were almost no capital funds on which to draw. The State Grant in Aid stood at £4,500. The College was taxed as a business on its small annual surplus. The chronic student was not unknown. The Faculties of Anaesthesia, Radiology and Dentistry were in their infancies.[26]

Rationalisation of medical education was discussed in Government and, in the absence of another Napoleon, state aid was not forthcoming. The School could build or close. The College embarked on a major development programme. The aims were to provide the most modern teaching facilities available at both undergraduate and postgraduate levels in an appropriate setting, while at the same time preserving the uniquely independent status of the College. Charitable status, following the example of the English College, was attained and fund-raising began.

The Appeal, launched in 1969, was directed towards graduates and fellows, parents and friends of the College, towards commercial firms, and in view of its international character, towards foreign governments whose citizens were represented in the student body. By the end of March 1981, £2 million had been generously subscribed by these sources—a practical demonstration of how many people shared the College's ideals of progress with independence.

Land to the rear of the College was bought and the development planned over three phases. The foundation stone was laid in 1974 for a new complex of lecture theatres, laboratories, student facilities and offices, 75,000 square feet in all. Cearbhall Ó Dálaigh, President of Ireland, opened the building on 27 April 1977. A second building, linking the old and new colleges, was completed in 1980.

Mercer Street revisited

In May of its Bicentenary Year, 1984, the College purchased Mercer's Hospital at a cost of £850,000. The development of this major acquisition was to provide student accommodation, a medical centre and a library. The façade of the old hospital was retained while all behind it was gutted and re-built. The Mercer's Medical Centre, having received its first patient on 17 September 1990, and the new RCSI Library were opened by Mary Robinson, President of Ireland, on 9 April 1991.

Overseas expansion

Recent years have seen an enormous expansion in the range, number and location of RCSI activities. In 2010, two hundred years after the opening of its first hall, the Royal College of Surgeons in Ireland incorporates Schools of Medicine, Pharmacy, Physiotherapy, Nursing and Healthcare Management. In addition, the College delivers postgraduate training and education in surgery and through its Faculties of Dentistry, Radiologists, Nursing and Midwifery, Sports and Exercise Medicine and the School of Postgraduate Studies. It conducts translational research through the RCSI Research Institute. More than sixty countries are represented in its international student body and the College is active abroad in the provision of education, training and hospital management with schools in Penang, Malaysia and Manama, Bahrain. The building of the new medical university in Bahrain, opened in 2009, is described by Colin Stewart in the final chapter of this book 'RCSI— Medical University of Bahrain, 2009'. In 2010, the current President, Professor Frank Keane, and Registrar, Mr Michael Horgan, step down and our first female President, Professor Eilis McGovern, and the new Registrar, Professor Cathal Kelly, begin the next chapter in the history of the Royal College of Surgeons in Ireland. It has started well, with independent degree awarding status being granted to the College on 12 October, 2010.

Notes

1 P. Crampton, *A lecture introductory to a course of clinical instruction delivered at the Meath Hospital and County Dublin Infirmary* (Dublin 1835) p 9 p 24.

2 J. D. H. Widdess, *The Royal College of Surgeons in Ireland and its Medical School 1784–1984* (Dublin 1984) p 85.

3 E. Mapother, 'Lessons from the lives of Irish surgeons—Address introductory to the session of the Royal College of Surgeons' in *Dublin Journal of Medical Science* vol 23 1873 pp 430–48.

4 RCSI College Minutes 4 February 1788.

5 Widdess op. cit. p 44.

Plate I: Portrait of George Renny by William Cuming 1810, oil on canvas (Courtesy Davison & Associates)

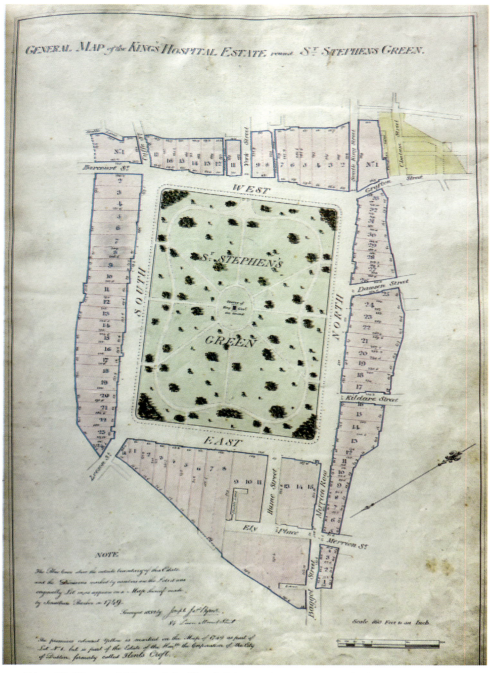

Plate II: 'General Map of the King's Hospital Estate round St Stephen's Green' by Joseph James Byrne, 1832 (The King's Hospital Archives, with thanks to the Board of The King's Hospital)

6 A. Colles, *A treatise on surgical anatomy (part the first)* (Dublin 1811) pp 24–5.

7 Ibid., p 26.

8 RCSI College Minutes 2 August 1819.

9 A. Colles, 'Second communication relative to the fatal consequences which result from slight wounds received in dissection' in *Dublin Hospital Reports* vol 4 1827 pp 240–4.

10 J. Houston, 'Observations on the mucous membrane of the rectum' in *Dublin Hospital Reports* vol 5 1830 pp 158–65.

11 MS RCSI Archives 1829 re Northumberland Wax Collection.

12 T. C. Lee, *Catalogue of the Northumberland Museum of the Royal College of Surgeons in Ireland* (Dublin 1992).

13 C. F. A. Marmoy, 'The Auto-Icon of Jeremy Bentham at University College London' in *Medical History* vol 2 no 2 1958 pp 77–86.

14 J. Cheyne, 'Case of apoplexy in which the fleshy part of the heart was converted into fat' in *Dublin Hospital Reports* vol 2 1818 pp 216–23.

15 A. Jacob, 'An account of a membrane in the eye, now first described' in *Phil Trans* vol 109 1819 pp 300–7.

16 C. A. Cameron, *History of the Royal College of Surgeons in Ireland, and of the Irish schools of medicine: including numerous biographical sketches, also a medical bibliography* (Dublin 1886) p 391.

17 A. Jacob, 'The introductory lecture delivered by Dr Jacob at the Royal College of Surgeons for the session, 1844–5' in *Dublin Medical Press* no 304 1844 pp 277–81.

18 J. B. Lyons, *A Pride of Professors: The Professors of Medicine at the Royal College of Surgeons in Ireland 1813–1985* (Dublin 1999).

19 Widdess op. cit. p 102.

20 RCSI Council Minutes 21 June 1888.

21 D. Mitchell, 'The Conjoint Board in Ireland "in retrospect" in *Journal of the Irish Colleges of Physicians and Surgeons* vol 16 1987 pp 82–4.

22 E. O'Brien, 'The Royal College of Surgeons in Ireland: A bicentennial tribute' in *Journal of the Irish Colleges of Physicians and Surgeons* vol 13 1984 pp 29–34.

23 R. F. Harrison, letter in *Journal of the Irish Colleges of Physicians and Surgeons* vol 5 1976 p 179.

24 H. O'Flanagan, 'Twenty years a' growing—The Royal College of Surgeons in Ireland from 1961–81' in *Journal of the Irish Colleges of Physicians and Surgeons* vol 11 1981 pp 53–62.

25 Widdess, op. cit. 'Easter Week, 1916, at the College' Appendix III pp 153–6, pp 154–5.

26 H. O'Flanagan, op. cit. p 53.

'Simply elegant'[1]—the original building of the Royal College of Surgeons in Ireland

Patricia McCarthy

With neither funds nor accommodation, the newly-chartered Royal College of Surgeons in Ireland held its first meeting in the Board Room of the Lying-in Hospital, now the Rotunda, on 2 March 1784. In May a committee was formed 'to enquire whether any and what building in this City would answer for a Hall for Carrying on the Business of this College, and upon what Terms such building may be obtained'.[2] Various possibilities were presented to the committee, such as a house in Golden Lane 'wherein the Lord Chancellor's Register now keeps his Office', and the 'Opera House, Caple Street'.[3] Finally, after their application for government funds was turned down by the Lord Lieutenant, it was resolved at a meeting on 4 April 1789, 'that a convenient place be provided and fitted up before 1st of October next, for the purpose of Anatomical Demonstrations and Dissections'.[4] In November, the College signed the lease for a piece of ground in Mercer Street, and the following year, as the international situation darkened, they received a government grant of £1000.[5]

The accommodation at Mercer Street was less than ideal. A plan of the College premises of 1810 shows a 'surgeons' theatre', part of a group of buildings, including a dissecting room, used by the College behind Mercer's Hospital (Fig. 1). Of two storeys, the ground floor accommodation included, in addition to the dissecting room, an office, a sitting room for professors and examiners, and other rooms. On the upper storey there was a theatre with semi-circular rows of wooden seats, a museum and a small preparation room.[6]

By 1804, as the global war between France and Great Britain entered its fifteenth year, it became obvious that the increase in the numbers attending rendered the accommodation at Mercer Street untenable, and

[15]

there was no space on which to expand. Another site, therefore, was required. At a meeting held on 16 February 1805, it was resolved:

> That a Plan and Estimate of a College this day submitted by Mr Assistant Renny be authenticated by the signature of the proper officers and transmitted to the Chancellor of the Exchequer of Ireland to be laid before Parliament. Resolved that the President, Secretary, and Messrs Renny, Stewart, McEvoy, Obré, Richards, Peile & Colles be a committee to enquire whether ground may be obtained in a proper situation to erect thereon a College and Theatre.[7]

At a further meeting on 8 June, Renny reported that 'a proposal had been made on this subject by the Society of Quakers', who had offered the site of their burial ground on St Stephen's Green to the College. It was decided that no time should be lost, that the committee should be empowered to come to an agreement with the Society for the purchase

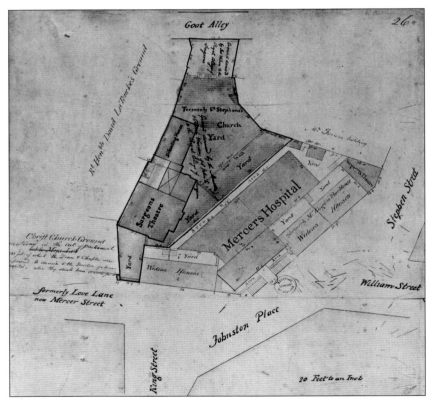

Fig. 1: *Plan of original College premises to the rear of Mercer's Hospital, 1810 (Longfield Collection, National Library of Ireland)*

of the site, and that it should 'be further impowered to draw the sum of £6000 voted in the present session of Parliament, towards the erection of said Hall and theatre from the Lords Commissioners of the Treasury'.[8] By 12 December 1805, the sum of 4,000 guineas had been paid to the Quakers for the site, which was described by the committee as 'very well adapted to the purpose being mainly in the centre of Dublin and at a short distance from Trinity College'.[9] With the site now acquired, the government was petitioned once more by the College for funds with which to build 'a Hall, Theatre, and Dissecting rooms for the use of this College', submitting the estimate for completing the buildings, amounting to £15,467. 10s. 7d. 'as laid before the College this day [12 December] by Edwd Parke, Esq. architect'.[10]

At a time when there was a choice of highly accomplished Irish architects working in Dublin, among them Francis Johnston and Richard Morrison, it seems rather puzzling that Edward Parke, an undoubtedly competent architect, but not one of the first rank, was handed such a prestigious commission. It would have seemed an ideal opportunity to hold a competition for the job, particularly as it was an institutional building funded by the government and located close to the centre of one side of St Stephen's Green. But, according to the minutes of the College, there was no debate about an architect, nor any alternative suggestions made. At the February 1805 meeting Renny had simply produced a plan and estimate that was immediately transmitted to the Chancellor of the Exchequer and, at the same meeting a committee was formed to find a site.[11] So even before they had procured a site for the College, the surgeons had their plan and, most likely, their architect.

George Renny (1757–1848) was responsible not only for the production of the plan, the estimate for the new building, and the purchase of the site, but he also managed to ensure a steady flow of funds from the government. He was Director General of the Army Medical Department in Ireland, and Surgeon to the Royal Hospital Kilmainham. Together with a number of other benefactors, he was responsible for the erection of forty street fountains, supplied with water from the Grand Canal, for the benefit of the poor of Dublin, and he was nominated by the Lord Lieutenant, Lord Hardwick as a member of a commission to enquire into the workings of the Paving Board. He was also, according to Charles

Cameron, 'an intimate friend of the Duke of Leinster whom he visited at Christmas over many years'.[12] Renny had, therefore, a considerable amount of influence in government circles at a time when there was a great demand for the training of military and naval surgeons due to the Napoleonic wars. An astute businessman, he was well placed to further the cause of the College of Surgeons, and this he did, very efficiently. As an acknowledgment of the debt they owed to him, in 1810 the College 'entreated' Renny to sit for his portrait, to thank him 'for his uniform and zealous exertions for the honour and advancement of surgery and for his able and successful representations to Government by which our applications to Parliament always met with the desired success whereby we have been enabled to erect our new Hall'.[13] The full-length portrait, painted by William Cuming (1769–1852), hangs in the Board Room, and shows Renny holding an architectural drawing of the front of the new building possibly taken from the brown portfolio at his feet (Plate I, page 11).

It can be assumed that the drawing is by Edward Parke. But by what criteria was Parke selected, and how did Renny come to present the College with almost a *fait accompli*? It might be interesting to speculate a little on these questions. But before doing so, a look at Parke and his career might be apposite.

Edward Parke, architect

Frustratingly, nothing is known of Edward Parke's early life or training.[14] The earliest we hear of him is that he was clerk of works to his father, Robert Parke (d. 1792), who was the superintending architect for the extension to the Irish House of Commons from 1787. Edward succeeded to this position on his father's death in 1792. He also succeeded his father as architect to the Dublin Society, and to the Linen Board. In 1795 he was admitted a Freeman of the City of Dublin as a member of the Corporation of Carpenters. The following year the erection of the Commercial Buildings on Dame Street began to Parke's designs. It was a prestigious commission, sponsored by many important merchants in the city who felt that space in the Royal Exchange for commercial transactions was limited and another city-centre location was required. Accordingly, a subscription to erect a suitable building was opened, shares of £50 each were issued to finance the project, and within a short time £20,000 had been collected. In 1796 building commenced and three years later it opened for business.[15] As late as 1844 Parke is listed as architect to the Commercial Buildings.

In about 1812 he was responsible for the building of farm offices and possibly a stable block at John Foster's residence, Oriel Temple in Collon, County Louth, and in the same county in 1813 he designed the Greek Revival County Court House in Dundalk. The commission for the courthouse was due to Foster, who was foreman of the Grand Jury and Governor of the county at the time.[16] The following year, however, Parke was dismissed from the latter commission as superintending architect, as he 'wishe[d] to have the appointment of individual artificers', terms that were considered 'inadmissable' by the Grand Jury overseers, and John Foster was requested to suggest some other architect to superintend the courthouse.[17] Parke was replaced by John Bowden. The courthouse, which is supposedly based on the portico design and dimensions of the Temple of Theseus in Athens, is an impressive classical building, starkly forbidding, with no applied decoration or openings in the façade save for the entrance (Fig. 2).

Fig. 2: County Courthouse, Dundalk, designed by Edward Parke, 1813 (Lawrence Collection, National Photographic Library, Dublin)

The name of John Foster (1740–1828) recurs in a number of Parke's commissions. Foster succeeded his father as MP for County Louth in 1768, a seat he retained until he became Lord Oriel in 1821. He became Chancellor of the Exchequer in 1784, Speaker of the House of Commons 1785–1800, and Chancellor of the Irish Exchequer at Westminster 1804–6 and 1807–11. The earliest link with Parke so far established was that of the Commons extension of the Parliament House in Foster Place (1787–93). James Gandon had been asked to supply drawings for that job, as his House of Lords extension on College Green was nearing completion, but Foster, as Speaker, and who presumably had the last word, did not approve of them. He was one of a group of Wide Streets Commissioners who attempted to thwart Gandon's efforts at every opportunity, and promote their own candidates. According to one writer, they were at a disadvantage with Robert Parke, who 'was of no consequence as an architect'.[18] As has been seen above, Edward succeeded his father in this commission in 1792.

It is likely that Edward Parke owed his position as architect to the Linen Board, one he claimed in 1829 to have had for nearly forty years, to Foster, who was interested in promoting the linen industry in Ireland, and was a trustee of linen manufacture in Ireland from 1779. In this capacity, Foster was able to disburse a great deal of patronage, mostly as a result of the 'inattention and bad attendance of almost all the members'; there was evidently no quorum.[19] According to the minutes of the Linen Board, at a meeting on 10 November 1801 only five of the seventy-two members were present. It was however acknowledged that the present accommodation was insufficient for their needs, and 'the Rt Hon Mr Foster having suggested to the Board a Plan for enlarging the said Hall by the addition of 80 or 100 rooms' it was resolved 'that the architect be directed to prepare plans'.[20] At the next meeting, on 8 December with eight members present, Foster produced a plan drawn by 'their architect' which was approved. At a following meeting on 25 January 1802 with four members including Foster present, the estimate was agreed and Parke was ordered to advertise in newspapers for proposals for prospective workmen. It is perhaps notable that Foster did not attend the next meeting of the board.[21]

In his various capacities, therefore, Foster had in his gift a number of jobs that he could disburse at will. According to Anthony Malcomson, he was 'strict in applying the criterion of efficiency' even in the most menial employee.[22] He probably found an efficient and reliable, if not exciting, architect in Parke, and their regular correspondence in which they exchanged notes about various commissions of Parke's, are peppered with expressions of the architect's gratitude for Foster's patronage.[23]

To return to the building of the College of Surgeons, it does not seem too wide of the mark to suggest that John Foster, Chancellor of the Exchequer during the crucial years of its construction, might have recommended to Renny the services of Edward Parke as the architect. For his part, Parke served the College well, providing them with an impressive building on a prestigious site.

Location

Eight years after its completion, in 1818, the new home for the Royal College of Surgeons in Ireland was described as

> well situated at the corner of York-street, the front facing St Stephen's Green. It is extremely well-built, the basement [ground-floor] story being of mountain granite, and the superstructure of Portland-stone; the façade is simply elegant, and ornamented with six columns of the Doric order.[24]

The new College and School undoubtedly occupied a prime site in the centre of Dublin on the west side of St Stephen's Green (Plate II, page 12). The name Frenchman's Walk was given to this side originally because of the number of French Huguenots who settled in the vicinity of the Green. Fleeing religious persecution in their own country, they were attracted to Ireland by legislation enacted in 1662 that encouraged Protestant strangers to settle here following the progressive dismantling of the tolerant Edict of Nantes, which was formally confirmed in 1685.[25] Street names in this area—Aungier, Digges—indicate their influence in the development of eighteenth-century Dublin and it is notable that, between 1708 and 1738, the Huguenots were involved in no fewer than seventy-one separate property transactions on all sides of the Green.[26] It is interesting, perhaps, to note that the Huguenots have to this day retained their graveyard on the north side of the Green, while the Quakers sold theirs to the surgeons for the building of their College and School.

[21]

St Stephen's Green was named after the church of St Stephen, the chapel of a leper hospital that dated from medieval times. It was a marshy common of about sixty acres, used by the citizens of Dublin as grazing land for their livestock. By 1664 a central area of twenty-seven acres, including the roadway, was to be preserved and ninety building lots around it, each with a frontage of about sixty feet, were distributed by ballot. The rent for each of these was to 'be disposed of for walling in the whole Greene and for paving the rodes or streetes'.[27] Each lessee was obliged to plant six sycamore trees near the wall, and ensure that they would survive for at least three years. There was no requirement to build, but if they did so, they agreed 'to build of brick, stone and timber, to be covered with tiles or slates, with at least two floores or loftes, and a cellar, if they please to digg it'.[28] These directions were sparse in comparison with those for the laying out of the later Georgian squares of Dublin, and perhaps it is not surprising that a visitor to Dublin, Richard Twiss, commented of St Stephen's Green in 1775: 'The houses in this square are so extremely irregular, that there are scarcely two of the same height, breadth, materials, or architecture'.[29]

In 1805, when the Quaker burial ground was acquired by the surgeons, the main entrance into the Green was opposite York Street, a gateway with 'four piers of black stone', each surmounted by a granite globe (see Fig. 11).[30] Because of this facility, it appears that houses were erected earlier on this side and on the north side of the Green than on the others but, while much re-building occurred in the mid-eighteenth century, when large mansions were built on the other sides, the same did not happen on the west side.[31] But the Green was a fashionable place in which to walk and be seen, particularly on the gravelled walk along the north side, known as Beaux Walk. Mrs Mary Delany, that great chronicler of eighteenth-century Dublin, was greatly impressed with it in 1731:

> As for Stephen's Green, I think it may be preferred justly to any square in London, and it is a great deal bigger than Lincoln's Inns Fields. A handsome broad gravel walk and another of grass, railed in round the square, planted with trees, that in summer give a very good shade; and every morning Miss Donnellan and I walk there.[32]

At least two prominent members of the RCSI were residents of

SIMPLY ELEGANT—THE ORIGINAL BUILDING OF THE RCSI

St Stephen's Green: Abraham Colles,[33] who lived on the north side at number 9, later moving to number 22, and James Henthorn, who lived at number 122 on the west side, just yards away from the College building. York Street, named after James II (1633–1701), who was created Duke of York and Albany as a child, was originally lined with town houses on both sides. As Mary O'Doherty has shown, it was a street that from the latter decades of the eighteenth century had numerous medical connections, not only private residences for doctors and surgeons, but also small hospitals and medical societies.[34] By the middle of the twentieth century these gracious Georgian houses had become tenements and were later demolished.

The Quakers

The site on which the surgeons would build their College was the 'ninth lott' of the west side, leased to William Anderson, a joiner, for the sum of £10. 3s. 6½d. in September 1664 and a yearly rent of £1. 0s. 4d. (Fig. 3). It measured 60 feet wide to the front and rear, 250 feet long on the

Fig. 3: Deed of conveyance of site on St Stephen's Green to William Anderson, 2 September 1664, with seal (Courtesy Davison & Associates)

[23]

north side and 238 feet six inches long on the south side. The following February, Anderson sold the site to William Starling, a tanner, for the sum of £32, who in turn sold it to a Quaker, Samuel Clarridge, in December 1666 for £37. 10s. od. The site remained in the possession of Quakers from then. Clarridge conveyed it to a miller, James Fade, for £40 who, in 1671, sold it to six trustees representing the Quaker community, 'that the said premises should and might from time to time during the will and pleasure of their friends (called the Quakers) in the City of Dublin be employed as burial ground for their said friends at their will and pleasure or the will and pleasure of any twelve or more of them'.[35] Abstracts of Quakers' wills show that the burial ground, which is clearly seen on John Rocque's map of Dublin of 1756, was used up to the middle of the eighteenth century.[36] Isaac Ashton of Kevin Street, Dublin stated in his will dated January 1755 that his body was

> to be decently buried in the quietest manner . . . by my dear wife's coffin on the left hand between hers and the South Wall, and full as deep in the Burial Ground of the people called Quakers near Stephen's Green, Dublin, in our family burial ground on the south side, as it is marked on the said wall by the letters T.A. cut in the stone of the said wall.[37]

The deed of conveyance in 1805 to the College of Surgeons stipulated that the purchaser 'under the penalty of Two thousand pounds Sterling . . . shall not nor will not at any time during the space of one hundred years from the date hereof raise or dig up for any purpose whatsoever' a part of the plot fifty-six feet wide and one hundred feet long, situated eighty-three feet back from the front on St Stephen's Green (Plate III, page 29).[38] The agreement seems to have been honoured up to 1875, when the College was planning to extend their buildings onto that area. Probably on legal advice, the College entered into an agreement with the Society of Friends at this time that any remains found on that ground be re-interred 'in some portion of the reserved ground and that the superfluous earth be carted by the authorities of the College, either to Cork-street or Temple-hill Friends' Burial Ground'.[39]

The new College building

One month after the laying of the foundation stone, on 10 April 1806, the building committee, with Dr Renny in the chair, and Edward Parke in attendance, agreed to 'the most advantageous proposals' put forward by a number of tradesmen for the building of the College and school. Some of the names, such as William Pemberton, bricklayer;[40] James Cockburn[e], stonecutter;[41] and Edward Robins, plasterer and painter,[42] were associated with Parke previously at the Linen Board. Others included John Peile, ironmonger, Thomas Delany, carpenter, George Elliot, slater, Nathaniel Walker, glazier and John Mallet, plumber. It appears from the minutes that Parke himself acted as building contractor, in receipt of proposals from individual tradesmen, as he had at the Linen Board. It was not unusual that architects brought their favourite workmen with them from one job to another. James Gandon brought his with him from his building of the Custom House, beginning in 1781, to his final public building, the King's Inns, begun in 1800, but he was not in receipt of a contractor's percentage.[43] As has been seen, in 1813 the Grand Jury overseers at Dundalk courthouse objected to Parke's perceived interference in this regard, when they probably preferred to invite competitive tenders, based on plans and specifications, from a number of general building contractors.[44]

Building probably commenced in June 1806 and continued to March 1810. By July 1809 the College, requiring land for 'burying dead bodies and other purposes and accommodations necessary to enable [them] to conduct an extensive Dissecting School placed in the centre of the city of Dublin' requested the exchequer for 4,000 guineas with which to purchase 'a lot of ground adjoining the College' that was sixty feet wide and 250 feet to the rear. The site, on which two houses were built was owned by James Lyne and was next to Glover's Alley. The houses were demolished and the materials salvaged and sold by Parke as the contractor for £34. 14s. 5d. A high wall now enclosed the new ground, and an entrance from Glover's Alley ensured that the 'business' connected with a school of surgery could be conducted 'with that secrecy and decorum which the nature of such institution ... requires'.[45] The wall, with a tree peering over the top, and the archway into Glover's Alley, can be seen in George Petrie's drawing of the College dated 1821 (half-title, page i).

The regularly-disbursed grants from Parliament for the building amounted to £29,104. 7s. 2d. and Parke was paid £1,421. 0s. 7d. commission as architect (Fig. 4). At a College meeting held on 2 May 1808 it

[25]

was resolved to send a letter to the Chancellor of the (Irish) Exchequer, John Foster, to thank him for his 'continuing patronage'.[46]

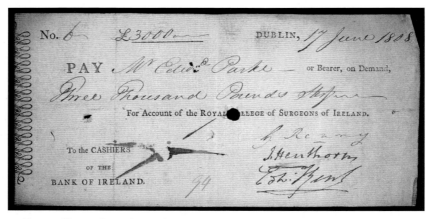

Fig. 4: Cheque from the RCSI drawn on the Bank of Ireland, and made out to Edward Parke, dated 17 June 1808

No original plans of the building survive, but by putting together pieces of information, it is hoped to reconstruct it as closely as possible. The anonymous print dated 1810 shows the building at an angle from across the road at St Stephen's Green (front cover). It shows the York Street façade, the wall behind which lay the school, and beyond that the tall residences. One bay of the house on the opposite side of York Street can be seen and, on the other side of the College are two houses. The first, a five-bay townhouse with Dutch Billie's roofline, and the other, probably of three bays, next to Glover's Alley. The drawings made by William Murray in 1825 for extending the building yield considerable information on the plan of the original College, and with the help of the College's minute books, the original room names can be ascribed to certain spaces, though the allocation of these spaces was not finalised for some years.[47]

The façade overlooking the Green was three bays wide, with two storeys over a basement, and built of Wicklow granite. A pediment, the full width of the façade, was supported by an entablature and six Tuscan columns, paired at each end, and one to each side of the central window of the *piano nobile*. The pediment, columns and probably the string-courses, were of Portland stone. [48] The rusticated ground floor had central and end projections on which the bases of the columns lay. However, these projections were not reflected in the entablature, something that would have been more correct and would have given the building a sense of movement. The large, round-topped windows of the *piano nobile* were set within relieving arches that sprang from a stone string-course. The windows that flanked the entrance door were almost square, while the doorway itself was generously wide with a segmental fanlight. The entablature, with a parapet above the cornice, continued along the five-bay York Street façade that is also rusticated at ground floor level. Here, however, the treatment of the fenestration is quite different. Above each of the five blind rectangular windows, and resting on a platband, are lunette windows, treated alternately with semi-circular architraves and, on a slightly smaller scale, set within a recessed rectangle, that give the false impression of a third storey behind. Further along this façade is a high wall of seven bays behind which the School was located. The 1810 drawing does not show the entrance to the School from York Street, but one is clearly seen in a later drawing of 1828, together with Edward Parke's earlier School buildings.

The motif of a window set within a relieving arch was one that found much favour with James Gandon, whose public architecture dominated Dublin for the last two decades of the eighteenth century and, with the King's Inns, into the early nineteenth century. It is probable that some of Gandon's work would have had an influence on Edward Parke. There is a certain affinity between the York Street façade of the College of Surgeons and that of the courtyard of the King's Inns, though Gandon locates *oeil-de-boeuf* windows along the upper part of his courtyard façade and a Diocletian window (rather than lunette) to the rear of the building.

Ground floor

From Murray's earliest drawing for the ground floor, dated 9 April 1825, the outline of Parke's building is quite clear (Fig. 5). Approached by three stone steps from the Green, the entrance hall to the centre of the building was quite a plain space with a broad arch to the rear leading into the back hall with the main staircase to the right. There were four doorways in the hall: two led to spaces to the left of the entrance, on the

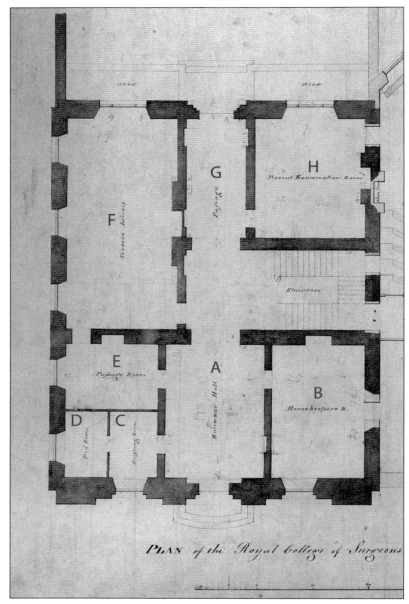

Fig. 5: Detail of plan by William Murray, dated April 1825, showing the ground floor of the 1810 building (Courtesy Davison & Associates).
Legend: A Entrance Hall; B Housekeeper's room;
C Dressing room; D Bedroom; E Passage room; F Present Library;
G Passage; H Present Examination room.

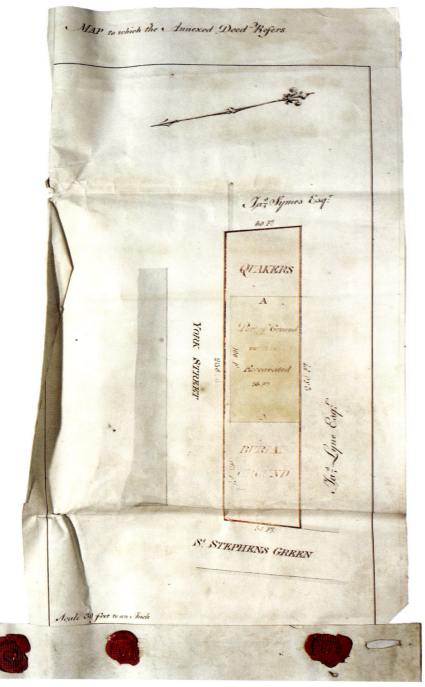

Plate III: Plan of site showing Quaker burial ground, from deed of conveyance to RCSI, 1805 (Courtesy Davison & Associates)

*Plate IV: Boardroom, spanning the width of the 1810 building
(Courtesy Davison & Associates)*

*Plate V: 'The Anatomy Lesson of the Irish College of Surgeons' by Robert Jackson, 2009
oil on canvas*

right was a dummy doorway (for symmetry), and the fourth led into a large room.[49] Beyond the arch and to the left, on the York Street side, was the three-bay library, with a tripartite or Wyatt window overlooking the yard and the School to the rear, and a fireplace. To the right was the stone, cantilevered staircase leading to the first floor, and behind this another room with a tripartite window to the rear. The entrance hall, together with the passage behind it, formed a corridor leading to the rear entrance to the building from the yard.[50] There were no fireplaces in the hall, nor in the two small rooms on its left to the front.

Decisions on the functions of these rooms were resolved, for the time being, in May 1809, and the furniture allotted the following September.[51] The front room off the hall to the left was to be 'allotted to the accommodation of the Professors' (on Murray's drawing of April 1825 it is annotated combined 'Dressing room' and 'Bed room'), furnished with a table and six chairs of mahogany, and the floor 'to be matted'. The room behind ('Passage Room') was to be an office for the secretary also with six chairs, an office table with drawers, fire irons and fender, and to be similarly floored. In the hall were another half dozen chairs[52] and a lantern there, and on the staircase.[53] The room on the right was a waiting room with twelve chairs and a table of mahogany, and was to be carpeted. The library was furnished with a large library table, reading desks, chairs and a commode, all of mahogany, and was to be 'covered with fine matting or oiled cloth'.[54]

First floor

Murray's drawings of the first floor show the Board Room occupying the full width of the three-bay building: it is of double height with a shallow segmental vaulted ceiling (Fig. 6). The two bays seen on the outside overlooking York Street are blank. The room has two fireplaces and doorways that are quite low for such a lofty space. It was to be furnished with a 'large elevated armchair for the President', thirteen armchairs, two semicircular mahogany tables and a square table 'to the ends of which the semicircular tables may be occasionally attached'. The table and some of the benches, made by John Davis, remain in the Board Room, but the clock, supplied by Frederick Hodges for thirteen guineas, was later moved to the Dissecting Room.[55]

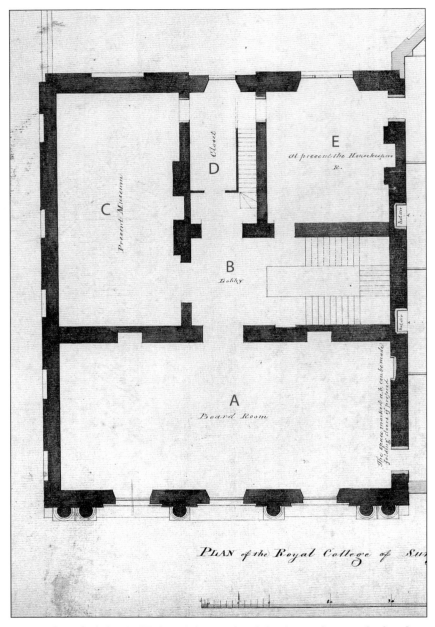

Fig. 6: Detail of plan by William Murray, dated April 1825, showing the first floor of the 1810 building (Courtesy Davison & Associates).
Legend: A Board Room; B Lobby; C Present Museum; D Closet; E At present Housekeeper.

SIMPLY ELEGANT—THE ORIGINAL BUILDING OF THE RCSI

From the lobby at the top of the staircase, double doors lead into the museum (also of two storeys), located above the library, where the three rectangular windows along York Street are blank, as is the end window: such openings would have limited exhibition space in the museum.[56] An interesting drawing by Murray dated December 1830 (Fig. 7), annotated 'A plan and Sections for fitting up the old Museum . . . for an addition to the Library', reveals that the original ceiling was barrel-vaulted, with transverse bands of Greek-key fretwork rising from between the lunettes. Here the three lunettes are framed within recessed rectangles, a pattern repeated in plaster on the other side of the room, and a large lunette over the tripartite window that overlooked the School. As can be seen from the drawing, the original window was reduced in size to facilitate shelving.

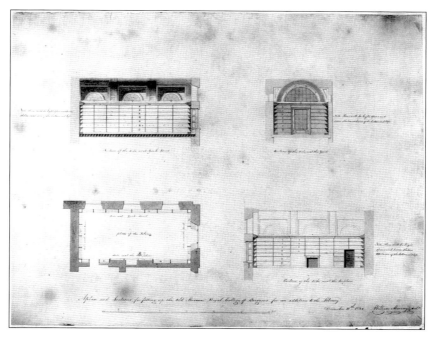

Fig. 7: 'A plan and sections for fitting up the old Museum . . . for an addition to the Library' by William Murray, December 1830

Two oval tables and a dozen chairs were allocated to the museum. Like the library, the floor covering in the Board Room and the museum was to be of matting or oiled cloth. A small storeroom off the museum,

[33]

and a narrow staircase leading to an attic storey, occupy the centre bay to the rear of the building and next to it a room with a tripartite window. No names were given to the rooms opposite the library on the ground floor, nor opposite the museum on the first floor, marked on Murray's drawings 'Present Examination Room', and 'at present the Housekeeper's room' respectively, but the minutes state that any apartments 'which are not allotted to a specific purpose in the foregoing resolutions, including the entire of the underground storey' shall be for the accommodation of a resident officer of the College and servants.[57]

Decoration

Many changes have been made to the 1810 building over the years but there are a few spaces that can still be attributed to Parke, such as the old hall and the Board Room, that have retained some of their decorative details. While the staircase would appear to be Parke's, the decoration seems to be by another hand.

Where an architectural order was used in a hall, it was typically that of the Doric, as here, in Parke's original hall, where there is a continuous frieze of alternate bucrania (ox skulls) and festoons or garlands, the latter quite thickly modelled (Fig. 8). The frieze is repeated in the lobby area of the stair hall beyond the arch,[58] where there is there is a pretty garland of acorns and oak leaves around the ceiling rose. The hall itself must have been quite dark, with light coming only from the fanlight,[59] but there was no such problem in the stair hall where the generous lantern provided a great deal of light. Yet more light comes through a second lantern over the upper landing ('Lobby'), outside the Board Room. The ceiling of the Board Room is decorated in the neoclassical style with some unusual motifs, like the bands of circles and part-circles (Plate IV, page 30). The low height of the doorways has been noted, and it can be assumed that the double doors to the left on entering, leading into the 1825 extension, were copied from the existing door from the landing, together with the very broad band of oak leaves in the frieze.

There are a few problems with the staircase and upper landing. To begin with the landing, a doorway is clearly marked on all of Murray's first-floor drawings that leads from the 'lobby' into the room behind the staircase ('housekeepers room'). It is to be seen also on Millar &

[34]

Fig. 8: Detail of frieze in entrance hall, and on staircase hall at ground-floor level (Courtesy Davison & Associates)

Symes' drawing of the first floor dated 1875[60] and was presumably blocked off when it was decided to move their rather inappropriate Ruskinian Gothic[61] opening in the stair hall (Fig. 9) from ground-floor level (Fig. 22), where it would seem rather awkwardly-positioned, to the first floor. The purpose of the opening was to provide light for a new, small staircase behind the main stairs, the former replaced at a later date with a corridor linking the new museum to Parke's building. With an amount of intervention on that wall—blocking a doorway and creating the opening—it would have been necessary to re-plaster it. While it is likely that Parke would have applied some stucco decoration in the stair hall, it may not have been similar to that currently on the walls, referred to by Christine Casey as having 'more than its share of husk garlands'.[62] In the opinion of one expert, the style of the decoration here appears to be later, probably dating to the Adam Revival, which began in the 1860s.[63] It would also seem fairly likely that the rest of the decoration in this area, including that around the lantern, was also executed during the 1870s work.

*Fig.9: 'Ruskinian' opening on main staircase wall
(Courtesy Davison & Associates)*

The school buildings

Unfortunately it is more difficult to reconstruct the school buildings to the rear of the College: that area was not part of William Murray's remit. But some idea of their layout in 1825 is found in a couple of his drawings that show the College separated from the school by a courtyard, access to which was through a gateway on York Street. Next to the gateway, on the inner wall, was a two-room porter's lodge (Fig. 10). The building marked 'Theatre &c', was of five bays, approached by three steps through a doorway flanked by engaged columns. A narrow passage divided this building from the 'Preparation Rooms &c', including Dissecting Rooms, built on the adjoining properties purchased by the College from James Lyne.

According to the minutes, the accommodation at the school was to consist of an anatomical lecture theatre, one public and one private dissecting room,[64] a preparation room and probably one or two store rooms. In January 1808, during the course of building, it was found that, due to 'the great increase of pupils', the dissecting room was to be extended by ten feet, and a gallery with stone staircase erected in the anatomy theatre, 'for the admission of strangers to witness the dissection of the bodies of such malefactors as may be executed for murder and sentenced to be publicly dissected'.[65] In 1810 the accounts show that £28. 8s. 9d. was paid 'for a table made on a particular construction for demonstrations and lectures in the Theatre of Anatomy'.[66] By the end of 1811, however, and with numbers of students continuing to grow, it became evident that additional dissecting rooms were necessary. Accordingly, the following year the construction of 'extensive' dissecting rooms, plus 'a theatre for anatomical demonstrations in the ground adjoining the College on St Stephen's Green', was well underway.[67] The buildings, executed by Edward Parke, were complete by January 1814, when Parke's association with the Royal College of Surgeons ended.

A description of the school buildings published in 1818 gives another insight into them:

> The theatre in which the lectures are delivered is capable of accommodating between 300 and 400 students, besides what the gallery may contain, which is opened for the public during the dissection of malefactors. Adjoining the theatre are the professors' dissecting room, and two museums ... the dissecting

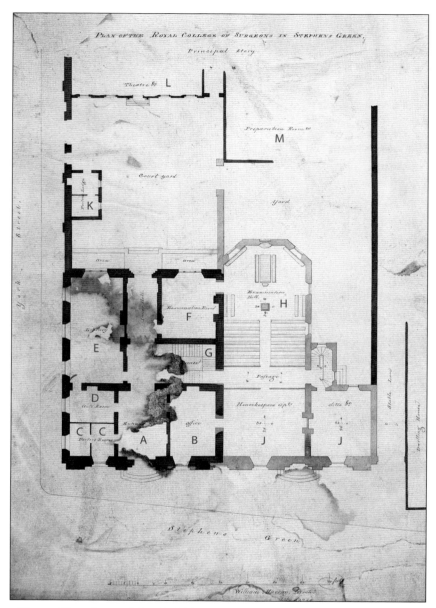

Fig. 10: Plan of ground floor by William Murray, 1825, showing location of School buildings to rear of Parke's College, with porter's lodge on York Street. Legend: A Entrance hall; B Office; C Porter's rooms; D Anti room; E Library; F Examination room; G Staircase; H Examination hall; J Housekeeper's apartments; K Porter's lodge; L Theatre &c.; M Preparation room &c.

rooms are very commodious, and were added but lately to the building. They consist of a public and private dissecting room, with suitable apartments and lofts for making and drying preparations. The public dissecting room is furnished with twenty tables, at each of which two students are placed. There is, moreover, adjoining, a theatre for demonstration, which may contain upwards of 100 spectators.[68]

In 'The Anatomy Lesson of the Irish College of Surgeons' (Plate V, page 30) the 1812 Dissecting Room that forms the southern third of the current Anatomy Room, can be seen on the left of the painting. The architects T. N. Deane & Son extended the room in 1891–2, to Glover's Alley on the north, where the new external wall with large windows was built. In the minutes of the College there is no mention of when the octagonal dissecting room seen on an 1832 plan was built, but it is likely to have been part of the 1812 additions mentioned above as 'added but lately to the building' (Fig. 11). During the period 1803 to 1816, the architect Richard Morrison was constructing Sir Patrick Dun's Hospital in Dublin where, to the rear of the central portion of the building, he designed a semi-circular theatre. The design was apparently derived from Jacques Gondoin's semi-circular, toplit, anatomy theatre at the École de Chirurgie, now École de Médecine, Paris (1769–75),[69] though the theatre in Mercer Street had semi-circular wooden seating in 1796.

It will be noted that, as well as the museum on the first floor in the College building, there were two smaller museums attached to the School. One of these was probably the stable and coach house erected in the grounds originally by the assistant secretary of the College, C. H. Todd, for his own use and at his own expense, in 1811.[70] Ten years later the minutes state that it was to be converted into a laboratory,[71] while Cameron contends that it became the 'school museum'.[72] Museums of anatomy, natural history and pathology were essential for the study of medicine in the nineteenth century, and the RCSI was continually adding to its collections. Apart from anatomy and pathology specimens, the collection consisted of items such as the skeletons of an Irish elk and an elephant, and the skulls of a giraffe, a hippopotamus and a narwhal's tusk.

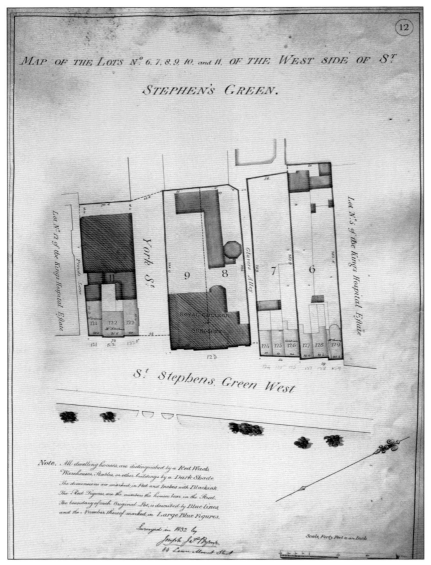

Fig. 11: Map showing RCSI property on Lots 8 and 9 St Stephen's Green, 1832. Note octagonal dissecting theatre (The King's Hospital Archives, with thanks to the Board of The King's Hospital, photo, author).

Surgeons' halls in Britain

The English surgeons had separated from the Guild of Barber-Surgeons in 1745, almost forty years before their counterparts in Ireland. For their early building they chose a site in London next to Newgate Prison, on what is now the Central Criminal Court in the Old Bailey.[73] Plans from William Kent (*c.* 1685–1748) and George Dance the elder (1695–1768) were dismissed as too expensive, and William Jones (d. 1757), who had designed the Rotunda in Ranelagh Gardens, Chelsea, secured the contract.

Having acquired funding from Parliament to purchase a bequest of 14,000 specimens, dissections and notes, in 1799 they acquired 41 Lincoln's Inn Fields. One of the stipulations of the bequest was that the surgeons must build a museum to house the collection and in 1802 they purchased 42 Lincoln's Inn Fields. Plans were drawn up by George Dance the younger (1741–1825) and James Lewis (*c.* 1751–1820),[74] with the government providing funds. Building began in 1805, the same year that the Dublin surgeons acquired the site on St Stephen's Green, and was complete in 1813, three years after the completion of the Irish building. Twenty years later, in 1833, Sir John Soane (1753–1837), architect to the College, uncovered serious structural defects in the building that necessitated almost complete reconstruction. To Soane's undoubted embarrassment, the competition for the job held that year was won by Sir Charles Barry (1795–1860) who would later build the Palace of Westminster and Houses of Parliament (1835–60). Barry was also the architect for the Travellers' Club in Pall Mall (1830–2) and, next door to it, the Reform Club (1838–41), both in the Italianate style. For the London surgeons, the acquisition of 40 Lincoln's Inn Fields enabled a much larger building to be planned. All that remained of Dance's building was the portico with its giant Ionic columns which were, like the Dublin College of Surgeons, realigned to fit in with the new extended façade. Much of Barry's building was destroyed by a German bomb in 1941, but the portico, library and entrance hall survive.

Like their Irish counterparts, the Scottish surgeons had lived a peripatetic life for many years; originally they used rooms in members' houses, then rented a few rooms in various tenement buildings, until in the mid-seventeenth century they moved into a large four-storey house with a garden where they could grow medicinal herbs. By 1697 a Surgeons' Hall had been built on the site, of nine bays and two storeys with 'semi-octagonal towers at the ends'. But the surgeons ran into financial difficulties almost immediately and had to rent out much of the accommodation. In the course of disposing of much of their land around the Hall, the area became known by 1786 as Surgeons' Square, 'the cradle of modern surgery in Edinburgh'.[75] However, by the early nineteenth century, the Surgeons' Hall was becoming inadequate for their needs and in 1822 they consulted the well-known Scottish architect William Playfair, 'whose elegant buildings were in exactly the sort of style and configuration which would enhance the status of the College'.[76] After numerous discussions and proposals, a site in Nicolson Street, formerly occupied by the Royal Manège (a riding school), was acquired and the foundation stone laid on 3 March 1830. The Greek Revival temple-style building has a forty-feet wide pedimented portico of six Ionic columns, the depth of the building was 190 feet, and it cost £13,257. 18s. 7d. Playfair also designed the interior, together with furniture and fittings for all the ground-floor rooms to give the scheme a coherence.[77] The College has remained at this location and, over the years, similar to its Dublin counterpart, has added to its accommodation.

The 1810 building extended

From around 1817 the condition of the museum in the RCSI's School buildings was being called into question. At a meeting in May 1819 it was stated that the room was unfit for the purpose for which it was intended, that many valuable preparations were in a state of decay, some having been destroyed by damp and lack of ventilation. It was resolved that the architect Francis Johnston should inspect the building and report back,[78] but nothing further was minuted on the subject. By November 1823 it was apparent that there was insufficient exhibition space in the museum, this time in the College building, to facilitate the increasing numbers of preparations that were being acquired. More space was needed 'which can be obtained by a new building or a judicious alteration of the present Board Room'; it was decided to consult 'with competent persons' on the matter among whom was Johnston, and to offer fifty guineas for the best design to be approved by the College.[79] The Curators of the Museum were keen that the addition of a new room should be 'on an extensive scale' and proposed that not just a new room, but a new building

> shall be erected on the ground between the College and Glover's Alley, with an handsome front to St Stephen's Green, if possible to correspond with the present front of the College, that the Museum shall occupy the second floor of said building, and that the first floor shall be constructed with a view to its future appropriation as an Examination Hall.

Francis Johnston (1760–1829), one of Ireland's foremost architects, had been responsible for numerous important commissions including the Chapel Royal at Dublin Castle (from 1807), St George's Church, Hardwicke Place, Dublin (1801) and the conversion of the Irish Parliament building on College Green into the Bank of Ireland (1803). He was one of the fourteen founder members of the Royal Hibernian Academy, incorporated in 1821, and became its President in 1824. At his own expense, he designed and built the Academy's premises in Abbey Street, Dublin (1824–6), which he leased to the Academy at a nominal rent.[80] William Murray (1789–1849), a cousin of Johnston's, designed a statue gallery at the Academy for Johnston's widow, Ann, in 1829.

It is not clear why the surgeons seem to have made no approach to Edward Parke at this point, as he would have been an obvious choice. He was still practising architecture and was, in 1825, working on the conversion of Moira House on Usher's Quay for the Dublin Mendicity Institution. Nonetheless, Johnston would probably have been their first choice of architect for the commission, not least because his younger brother, Andrew Johnston, was a member of the College, becoming its treasurer in 1820.[81] It seems his workload and failing health precluded him. The College asked him to recommend a substitute and he proposed his assistant William Murray. It is evident that Johnston was retained as consulting architect for the job.[82]

Murray had joined Johnston's office in 1807. By then Johnston was architect to the Board of Works and in 1822 Murray became his assistant. It is notable that between 1824 and 1827 both men were referred to as 'Joint Architects and Inspectors of Civil Buildings'. Due to ill-health and, as has been suggested, partly 'as a revolt against the type of commissions he received in his position as architect of the Board of Works, which was basically unsuited to the sensitivity of his nature and style',

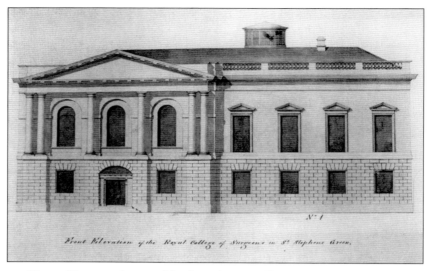

Fig. 12: Unexecuted proposal for front elevation, William Murray, April 1825.

Johnston resigned his position and in February 1827 Murray succeeded him.[83] In 1818, Murray was appointed architect to the Commissioners for Erecting and Establishing District Lunatic Asylums in Ireland, a position he retained until 1835. He was architect to the Royal Hospital at Kilmainham, and to the House of Industry, and he ran a successful private practice, taking his son, William George Murray, into it in 1845.

On 27 June 1825 Murray's designs were accepted, and another family tie was consolidated when the board accepted the tender put forward by the builders Messrs Murray & Dwyer: the Murrays were William's brothers, Edward and Arthur. Of the four tenders received, theirs was the second highest at £6047.[84] This was not necessarily nepotism: there was no reason why the College would do the Murrays a favour at a financial cost to itself.[85]

An early drawing prepared by Murray of the new front elevation shows a four-bay balustraded extension to the right of, and set back slightly from, Parke's building, with triangular pediments over the windows of the *piano nobile* (Fig. 12). Above the roof-line the first of four lanterns that provided light in the new museum on the first floor can be seen.[86] In a letter to the surgeons in April 1825, Murray set out his stall:

To make the building as distinct as the nature of the connexion with the existing front would admit of, secondly to keep down the expense as much as possible, but if it be the wish of the College to adopt a more costly arrangement and to have a uniform front this will be quite practicable, but of course the front of the present building will require to undergo a considerable alteration.[87]

By the end of July the drawings show a substantial alteration to the façade. Parke's original front was to be greatly extended towards Grafton Street, rearranging the original composition. The new building was to have seven bays as opposed to three. The centre of the building was to be shifted, from the point of view of a spectator in St Stephen's Green, to the right. One drawing shows the original entrance doorway and hall remaining where it was, and a dummy door for symmetry placed on the opposite side of the central axis. That was later changed to a doorway in the central bay and the original doorway replaced by a window (Figs 13, 14). The pediment was moved and relocated to the new centre. Murray also re-cycled Parke's columns, moving the single column and the pair of engaged columns on the right to a similar position to the right of

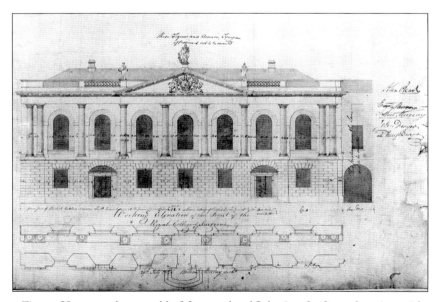

Fig. 13: Unexecuted proposal by Murray, dated July 1825, for front elevation with 'dummy' hall door to the right for symmetry, with plan for later (executed) façade at the bottom of the drawing. Note extension over Glover's Alley to right.

[45]

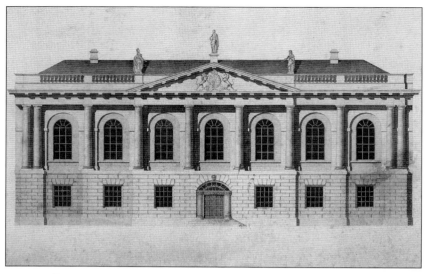

Fig. 14: Front elevation as built (Courtesy Davison & Associates)

the extended building, and adding four new free-standing columns to support the pediment.

This plan, which included building over the entrance to Glover's Alley, met with the approval of the College in July, but in September they abandoned the idea of building over the lane-way as there would be a risk of fire from neighbouring houses, and on the grounds that it would take from the 'appearance of the great front to the Green'.[88] The added cost of these changes from the original plans amounted to £338, making a total of £6,385.[89]

It is interesting to compare the early plans where it was proposed to retain the narrow hall of Parke's building as the entrance hall of the extended building (Fig. 10) with the later, July plan (Fig. 19), and the much grander hall that was actually executed (Plate VI, page 47 and Fig. 22).

The façade of the building was enhanced by the sculptural figures of Aesclepius, the Greek god of healing, on the apex of the pediment, flanked by Athena, the goddess of war and wisdom, on his right, and by Hygeia, goddess of health and healing, on his left. Within the pediment is a relief of the royal arms and, as a keystone over the arch of the (central) entrance doorway is the head of Aesclepius. All of the sculpture was

*Plate VI: Entrance Hall of College building
(Courtesy Davison & Associates)*

*Plate VII: Brass and wood lock on entrance door, typical of Irish Georgian houses
(Courtesy Davison & Associates)*

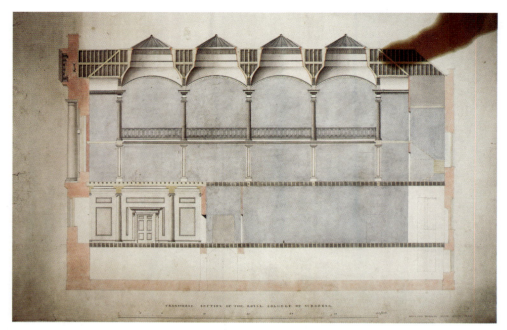

Plate VIII: Longitudinal section of William Murray's Examination Hall on ground floor, and Museum with gallery on first floor (Courtesy Davison & Associates)

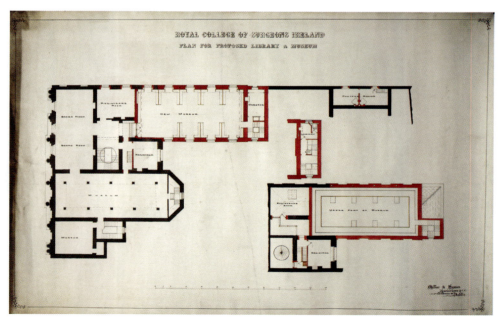

Plate IX: First-floor plan by Millar & Symes, c. 1875, showing new Museum, and upper part of same (Courtesy Davison & Associates)

created by John Smyth ARHA (c. 1773–1840), the son of Edward Smyth (who was responsible for much of the sculpture on Gandon's Custom House). He was paid £200 for the three figures and the royal arms, plus £10 for an assistant.[90]

The main doorcase is interesting. The earlier plan (Fig. 15) with, to each side, projecting paired pilasters topped by consoles, was abandoned.[91] In a finished, presentation drawing dated September 1827 (Fig. 14), and as built, (Fig. 16), the doorcase is quite different and derives from James Gandon via Francis Johnston. Gandon's piers to Carlisle (later O'Connell) Bridge in Dublin (1791–5), which can still be seen, have curved Portland stone panels attached, the bases of which are channelled and splayed, as on the doorcase.[92] A similar pattern can be seen on the gate piers of the City gate into Áras an Uachtaráin, formerly the Vice Regal Lodge in Phoenix Park, designed by Johnston in 1808 (Fig. 17). The design was

Fig. 15: Proposed entrance doorway, February 1826

thus reused to each side of the College doorcase, with the addition of the rather unusual Greek-key frieze that extends into rounded capitals. Just as Gandon placed a personification of the River Liffey as a keystone in the centre arch of the bridge, Aesclepius takes that position at the College doorway. It is likely that the brass and mahogany lock from the original door, typical of eighteenth-century Dublin houses, was re-used on the inside of the new door (Plate VII, page 47).

The balustrading on the building was extended, in 1827, to the flank of the College along York Street as the committee was of the opinion that

> it will not only add materially to the general character of the college as a great public building, but that the want of it will render it so defective in architectural uniformity and elegance that they anticipate the dissatisfaction of the members of the college at a future period.[93]

At the same time the wall of the College along York Street was 'scoured' and pointed, and an estimate for £84 was accepted from Messrs McKean & Goodwin for iron railings for the front of the College: the height of the railing to be five feet three inches and each rail to be without ornament.[94]

Fig. 16: Entrance doorway as executed (Courtesy Davison & Associates)

Fig. 17: Gate piers at Áras an Uachtaráin, by Francis Johnston, 1808 (Photo, author)

Interior

The plans drawn up in April 1825 show no intervention in Parke's building on either ground or first floor apart from doorways broken into the new extension (Figs 5, 6). On the ground floor the two new rooms to the front of the extension were for a housekeeper and for examination candidates, and on the upper floor the museum ran the full depth of the building, with a room next to it to the front (annotated on July plan 'Small museum') (Fig. 18) and, behind it, a staircase. The plan dated to July shows the old entrance hall, together with the three rooms behind the first bay, absorbed into a proposed extension of the library, making that an L-shaped space,[95] and a new proposed entrance hall taking up the central three bays (Fig. 19).

In 1827 Murray had second thoughts about the entrance hall that he had planned two years before, which was then to be 'fitted up plain', and sent the College a drawing

> for finishing the Entrance Hall the ceiling of which being very low it will be necessary to divide it into compartments to give the effect required and this will be most effectually attained by Columns and pilasters with an architrave and bold cornice.[96]

The hall, which bears a similarity to that of the Rotunda Hospital in Dublin, built from 1750, has four free-standing Ionic columns with respondent pilasters (Plate VI, page 47). Edward McParland has proposed that the lack of cohesion in the use of the order here would have been more successful had Murray placed the volutes on the diagonal (as in the present College Hall) or, better still, had he used the Doric order, as at the Rotunda.[97] Like the Board Room upstairs, the doors here could have been higher. The fretwork on the soffits makes a bold statement, and is not dissimilar to that in Francis Johnston's cash office at the Bank of Ireland (1804) and at St George's Church, Hardwicke Place in Dublin. The floor is of Yorkshire flagging and the niche opposite the hall door was for a stove with a Portland stone platform.[98]

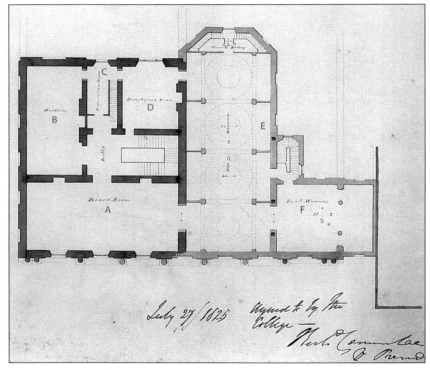

Fig. 18: Plan of first floor showing 'Small Museum' extending over Glover's Alley, July 1825.
Legend: A Board room; B Museum; C Preparation room; D Housekeepers room; E Museum; F Small Museum.

In Murray's July plan (Fig. 19), to the right of the hall was a one-bay porter's room and, next to it a room for the housekeeper. The new examination hall extended back from behind the entrance hall with a canted bay facing into the yard. Similarly on the first floor (Fig. 18) the new museum extends back from the front of the building by seventy feet (necessitating three blank windows on the *piano nobile* to facilitate exhibits). It was thirty feet wide and twenty-four feet high, lit by four large circular lanterns. The canted bay to the rear of the space, which contained the stairs to the gallery, was partitioned off with a central doorway. A section through the long axis of the museum shows five square piers to each side supporting the gallery, and above them, slender fluted Ionic columns with their own entablatures. A band of fret

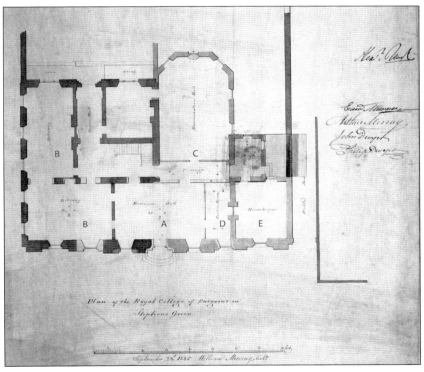

Fig. 19: Plan of ground floor showing library extended to front of building, July 1825 (Courtesy Davison & Associates).
Legend: A Entrance hall; B Library; C Examination hall; D Porters room; E Housekeeper.

extended from above the columns across the space between the lanterns (Plate VIII, page 48 and Fig. 20). In a letter to the College in December 1826, Murray was of the opinion that 'the Ionic columns of the galleries will be greatly improved by fluting their shafts which will cost about twenty pounds', and this was subsequently agreed to (Fig. 21).[99]

Prior to April 1825, Murray had been asked by the College for two estimates regarding the Board Room: one was to fit it up as a museum, the second as a library. His reply to the former was not favourable:

> In the first place this large room will require to be lighted by two or more lanterns and the present windows stopped up. The room is by no means calculated for setting lights on of the above description without a serious and expensive alteration; secondly the handsome cove ceiling would be destroy'd, and thirdly the external appearance materially injured by the lanterns which must be placed within six or seven feet of the front. I conceive it my duty to make the above observations previous to any arrangement.[100]

The estimate for the proposed conversion to a museum, which included a gallery supported on metal columns around the entire room, came to £385. 1s. 4d., and that for a library 'with plain shelving and fronts secured with green or scarlet stuff drapery' was £82. 16s. 10. Neither idea was pursued. However, as has been mentioned, in November 1830 Murray was asked to examine the old museum on the first floor in Parke's building with a view to converting it into an extension of the library (Fig. 7). His letter to the finance committee showed his reservation:

> I have viewed the panelled bands dividing the coved ceiling of the Old Museum, a part of which has been originally formed by brackets to complete the semicircle. I understand it has been proposed to take away the lower part and to leave the upper portion over the line of the horizontal Grecian frett. In my opinion if such an alteration be made the appearance of the room will be greatly injured.[101]

It is not clear what Murray meant by taking away the 'lower part': perhaps there was some sort of architectural articulation such as pilasters in the room. The following month, however, he produced the plans and, according to Cameron, 'the room formerly used to contain the Museum, which had now been removed to larger apartments, was in 1830 added to the library', which meant that the library was now located on both ground and first floors.[102]

[54]

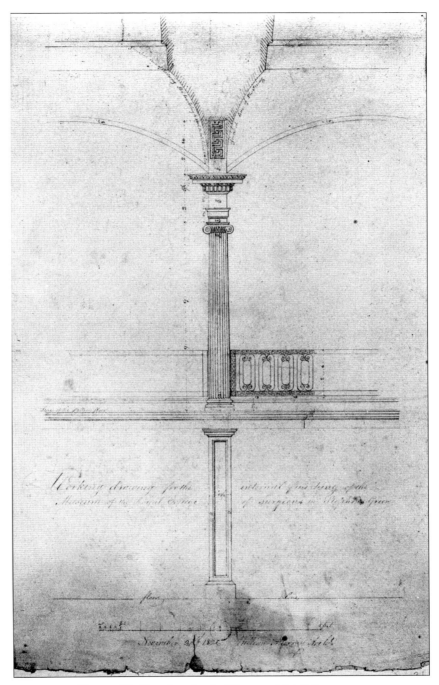

Fig. 20: Working drawing by Murray of detail for museum

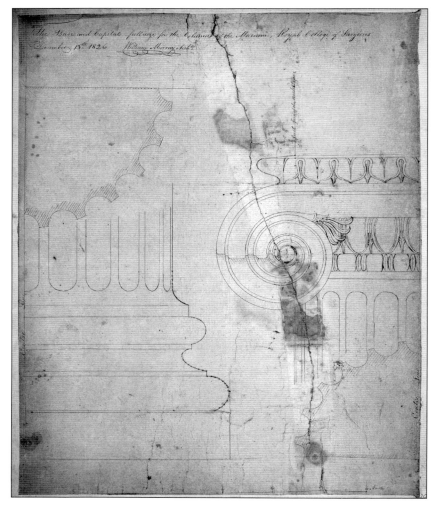

Fig. 21: Full-size drawing by Murray for base and capital of columns in museum, December 13, 1826 (Courtesy Davison & Associates)

Between 1875 and 1878 significant interventions into Parke's building included the idiosyncratic opening on the wall of the main staircase to provide light for a new staircase behind it, which was mentioned earlier. The architects Richard Chaytor Millar and William J. Symes (whose partnership was formed in 1873), were asked to prepare plans for 'enlarging the Museum and Library'. The museum at this time was that built from 1825, but any extension was problematic because of the building, in 1832, of a chemical lecture theatre and laboratory directly behind Murray's extension. The library was, as has been seen, located on two separate levels, which must have been less than convenient. So Parke's original plan of the museum over the library along the York Street façade was reverted to, but the façade was extended by eighty feet. This major intervention in Parke's building involved demolishing most of its rear wall, reducing the size of the three-bay rooms on the York Street side to two bays each, i.e. about twelve feet. This had the effect of providing extra width to both of the new spaces,[103] the library and the museum, and four bays matching Parke's were added along York Street (Fig. 22, Plate IX, page 48). To gain extra height for the ground-floor library, the level of the floor was lowered. The steps to this level can be seen in a photograph dating from 1908 (Fig. 23) looking towards Parke's building beyond the twin Ionic columns.[104] On the first floor the new, extended museum had a gallery all around it. The lunettes were blocked off, and the windows below opened. A partially-glazed ceiling, supported by exposed timber and iron trusses resting on somewhat out-of-place stone corbels, provided more light (Fig. 24).[105] As a postscript to this, yet more development was to occur in the museum: before 1915 the need for a new pathological laboratory was expressed, but the estimate was

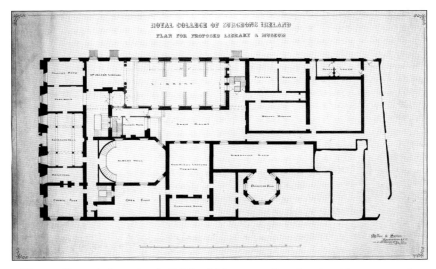

Fig. 22: Ground-floor plan by Millar & Symes, c. 1875, showing library extension along York Street (Courtesy Davison & Associates)

Fig. 23: Old photograph of the library extended by Millar & Symes, 1875–8, along York Street. Note steps to level of Parke's 1810 building.

Fig. 24: Old photograph of the first-floor museum extended by Millar & Symes, 1875–8, along York Street

apparently too high. The solution was found by inserting an entirely new floor into the museum, creating two storeys from the one space, the laboratory being located on the upper floor![106] In the 1990s, the lower floor was converted into offices while the upper floor now houses the Nightingale Theatre and the Newman Study.

The large museum designed by Murray had been converted, by 1905, into a new examination hall, known now as the College Hall. The galleries and other fittings were removed, leaving only the lanterns. It is used for College examinations and dinners. Below it, on the ground floor, the height of Murray's examination hall was considered too low in 1859 and the floor was sunk five feet into the basement. The death of Prince Albert, consort to Queen Victoria, who had visited the College in 1849, occurred during the renovation of the space in 1861, and it is now known as the Albert Theatre.

Conclusion

Although much of the original building has been subsumed into later additions, enough of it has survived to allow for tracing its growth and development into the complex of buildings that is the RCSI today. As has been seen, the institution, throughout its building history, continually needed extra space as student numbers, courses, books and museum items increased. That they never appeared to have too much trouble in raising the necessary funds was a tribute to their business acuity. The establishment of the College and School on St Stephen's Green owes much to Dr Renny who saw the opportunity, given the great need for naval and military surgeons during the Napoleonic Wars, to further the cause of the College. He was able to ensure, through his political contacts, a steady flow of government funding that benefited not only the College, and the armed forces, but also the people of Ireland.

The 1810 building for the Royal College of Surgeons in Ireland was more than just a structure: its importance lay in the fact that it has enabled the institution and its structures to grow in tandem over the past 200 years. It was not simply the prestige of a city centre site on which was erected a purpose-built College and School, but its symbolic value that was so important both for the members of the College and for the public's perception.

[59]

Acknowledgements

Colin Brennan's MA thesis on the architecture of the Royal College of Surgeons in Ireland proved a valuable resource in the preparation of this essay. Special thanks go to Edward McParland, Conor Lucey, Jeremy Williams, David Davison and Edwin Davison for their help. Mary O'Doherty, assistant librarian RCSI, was a joy to work with: her enthusiasm for the project, knowledge of the archive, and her valuable suggestions, have been much appreciated.

Notes

1   J. Warburton, J. Whitelaw and R. Walsh, *History of the city of Dublin* 2 vols (London 1818) ii p 753.

2   RCSI/COL/1, Minutes of College meetings, 2 March 1784–1 November 1802, meeting 15 May 1784.

3   RCSI/COL/1, meetings 10 July 1784 and 1 November 1784.

4   RCSI/COL/1, meeting 4 April 1789.

5   RCSI/COL/1, meetings 2 November 1789 and 9 March 1790.

6   J.D.H. Widdess, *The Royal College of Surgeons in Ireland and its Medical School 1784–1984* (Dublin 1984 ed.), p 25.

7   RCSI/COL/3, Minutes of College meetings, 7 January 1793–27 November 1810, meeting 16 February 1805.

8   RCSI/COL/3, meeting 8 June 1805.

9   According to Widdess, this probably indicated that many students from Trinity College made use of the facilities available in the surgeons' school. Widdess, p 62.

10   RCSI/COL/3, meeting 12 December 1805.

11   RCSI/COL/3, meeting 16 February 1805.

12   Sir Charles A. Cameron, *History of the Royal College of Surgeons in Ireland* (Dublin 1886) pp 320–1.

13   RCSI/COL/3, meeting 6 August 1810.

14   Biographical information on Edward Parke is from the database of Irish architects in the Irish Architectural Archive, www.dia.ie.

15   The building was demolished in 1973 to make way for the Central Bank.

16   *Dictionary of National Biography*.

17   Public Record Office of Northern Ireland, Foster/Massareene Papers, T.2519/4/1387 and /1390, Letter from Edward Parke to Robert Page, 16 September 1812; Letter from J. Jocelyn to John Foster, 18 September 1812.

18   Edward McParland, *James Gandon: Vitruvius Hibernicus* (London 1985) p 95.

19   A. P. W. Malcomson, *John Foster: the politics of the Anglo-Irish ascendancy* (Oxford 1978) p 270.

[60]

SIMPLY ELEGANT—THE ORIGINAL BUILDING OF THE RCSI

20 Parliamentary Papers Ireland, *Papers relating to linen and hempen manufacture in Ireland, Minutes of the Linen Board, 10 November 1801.*

21 Ibid., *Minutes of the Linen Board, 8 December 1801 and 25 January 1802.*

22 Malcomson, *John Foster* p 267.

23 PRONI, Foster/Massereene Papers, T.2519/4/1330, Letter from Parke to Foster 4 July 1812; D.207/28/640, Letter from Parke to Lord Oriel 16 November 1821.

24 Warburton, Whitelaw and Walsh, *History,* ii p 753.

25 Irish Statutes 14 and 15, Ch II, c 3.

26 Rowena Dudley, 'St Stephen's Green: the early years 1664–1730' in *Dublin Historical Record*, vol. liii, no 2, Autumn 2000 pp 157–79.

27 *St Stephen's Green, 1880–1980* (National Parks & Monuments Service 1980).

28 Maurice James Craig, *Dublin 1660–1860* (Dublin 1969) p 20.

29 Richard Twiss *A Tour in Ireland in 1775* (London 1776) p 12.

30 Quoted in *The Georgian Society Records* (Shannon 1969 ed.) ii p 40.

31 *The Georgian Society Records* ii p 98.

32 Angelique Day (ed), *Letters from Georgian Ireland* (Belfast 1991) pp 26–7.

33 Among the Longfield Maps in the National Library of Ireland is one showing 'Surgeon Collis [sic] holding', two adjoining houses on St Stephen's Green with a stable lane next to one, with stables and coach houses to the rear. NLI, Longfield Maps, 12F 90/206.

34 Mary O'Doherty, 'The medical connexions of Dublin's York Street', *Journal of the Irish Colleges of Physicians and Surgeons* vol 30 no 2 April 2001 pp 107–13.

35 RCSI Archives, Assignment of ground on St Stephen's Green, 2 February 1665 from William Anderson to William Starling.

36 According to *The Georgian Society Records*, 'the cemetery became disused except for occasional burials, at the end of the seventeenth century, the Quakers having formed a new burying-ground in Cork Street in 1697', ii p 101.

37 http://www.failteromhat.com/quaker/page1.php. Thanks to Mary O'Doherty for bringing this to my attention.

38 RCSI Archives, BF LO/An/1, deed of conveyance, 1805.

39 Cameron, *History* pp 238–9. Cameron states that the agreement was violated in 1825 and 1836 'when the buildings were extended' (p 142). This might refer to the relocation of the porter's lodge on that piece of ground in 1825, but it is not clear that there was any extension in 1836 when, he says, the Quakers considered taking action against the college but resolved instead 'in the interest of peace' to desist. Cameron also states that in 1876 the Council of the college were unaware of the deal with the Quakers and, on being informed, orders were given to stop the building to enable negotiations to take place. As one of the Quakers' rules advised 'that all friends be careful to avoid it with all persons, as much as may be, and endeavour to live at peace with all men; for we are called to peace, and to be

[61]

SURGEONS' HALLS

a peaceable people', it was probably unlikely that they would have pursued legal action.

40 William Pemberton (1751–1811), worked at the Tholsel in Dublin and tendered successfully to build the City Marshalsea (1803). IAA, http://www.dia.ie.

41 A John Cockburn died *c.* 1811–12, IAA, http://www.dia.ie.

42 Edward Robbins is listed in the IAA database as a plasterer and architect.

43 Patricia McCarthy, *'A favourite study': building the King's Inns* (Dublin 2006) p 32.

44 Colin Brennan, 'The Royal College of Surgeons in Ireland: an architectural history 1805–1997', unpublished MA thesis, University College Dublin, 1997, p 10.

45 RCSI/ COL/3, meeting 2 July 1809.

46 RCSI/COL/3, meeting 2 May 1808.

47 Cameron, *History* p 144.

48 Though in their description of the building in 1818, as has been seen, Warburton, Whitelaw and Walsh describe the lower part of the building 'of mountain granite and the superstructure of Portland-stone'; ii p 753.

49 As the functions of some of these rooms changed over the course of 1825 in Murray's drawings, the room names will be discussed below.

50 These combined spaces leading to the rear door would seem to have the 'speed and connectivity' that Professor Jarzombek associates with the corridor in his essay in this publication, as the College connects with the School behind it.

51 RCSI/COL/3, meetings 29 May 1809 and 23 December 1809.

52 Though '8 mahogany hall chairs' were ordered from John Davis on 29 September 1810. RCSI/FIC/1 22 November 1808–8 December 1818.

53 According to a writer in 1824 there was, by the staircase, 'of gigantic dimensions, a cameleopard' which, according to the *OED* was a giraffe, that had been presented to the College. Martin Fallon (ed), *The sketches of Erinensis* (London 1979), p 17.

54 From the early part of the eighteenth century these cloths were a popular and cheap substitute for carpets until the advent of linoleum in 1860. Made from wide sheets of seamless canvas which were stretched on a frame, they were painted on both sides with many layers of pigment mixed with linseed oil and left to dry for several months.

55 Widdess, *The Royal College* p 64–5.

56 According to Erinensis, the museum in 1824 had one window to supply the room with light. Fallon p 17.

57 RCSI/COL/3. meeting 27 June 1816, John Humphries was elected clerk and housekeeper at £50 p.a. plus an allowance for coal and candles.

58 This opening is no longer in the former hall, but an arched display cabinet has replaced it in the back hall. The frieze may not have continued into the space called on Murray's plan, 'Inner Hall' that seems to be separated from the back hall by another arch, and that leads to the back door of the building.

[62]

SIMPLY ELEGANT—THE ORIGINAL BUILDING OF THE RCSI

59 Erinensis said of the hall that 'with a little more elevation [it] would be grand'. Fallon p 17.

60 Where a back staircase has been inserted behind the staircase wall.

61 Christine Casey, *The buildings of Ireland: Dublin* (New Haven and London 2005) p 484.

62 Ibid.

63 My thanks to Dr Conor Lucey for his opinion on the plasterwork.

64 RCSI/COL/3, meeting 23 December 1809.

65 RCSI/COL/3, meeting 13 January 1808. The gallery and stairs were described as 'Mountain stone gallery, iron railing & oak handrail' with '2 mountain stone stairs for ingress and egress', the cost for which amounted to £561. 0s. 0d., according to Parliamentary Papers 1808.

66 RCSI/FIC/1 22 November 1808–8 December 1818, meeting 23 June 1810.

67 RCSI/COL/4, Minutes of College meetings 7 January 1811–13 December 1824, meetings 4 December 1811, 4 May 1812 and 3 October 1812.

68 Warburton, Whitelaw and Walsh, *History* ii, pp 751–2.

69 Ann Martha Rowan (ed), *The architecture of Richard Morrison and William Vitruvius Morrison* (Irish Architectural Archive 1989) p 80–1. My thanks to Dr Edward McParland for this reference.

70 RCSI/COL/4, meeting 4 February 1811. This was permitted as he was resident officer in the college.

71 Ibid., meeting 5 February 1821.

72 Cameron, *History* p 276.

73 The information on the London College is informed by John P. Blandy and John S. P. Lumley (eds), *The Royal College of Surgeons of England: 200 years of history at the Millennium* (London 2000).

74 James Lewis provided several plans for buildings in Ireland in his *Original designs in architecture, consisting of plans etc, of villas, mansions, town houses etc.*, 2 vols (London 1779/80 and 1797).

75 Quoted in Helen M. Dingwall, *'A famous and flourishing society': the history of the Royal College of Surgeons of Edinburgh 1505–2005* (Edinburgh University Press *c.* 2005) p 274. This publication informs the account here of the Edinburgh College.

76 Ibid., p 275. Playfair (1790–1857) had designed numerous streets in Edinburgh and some of that city's finest buildings, such as the Greek Revival Royal Scottish Academy (begun 1822) and later the Neoclassical National Gallery of Scotland (1850–7).

SURGEONS' HALLS

77 William Playfair designed Drumbanagher House, County Armagh in *c.* 1833 for Maxwell Close, brother-in-law of the 1st Lord Lurgan, and dining room furniture for it. He sent over full-size drawings for a chair preferring to 'leave nothing to the imagination of an Irish tradesman'. Patricia McCarthy, unpublished PhD thesis, 'The planning and use of space in Irish houses 1730–1830', Trinity College Dublin 2009, p 123.

78 RCSI/COL/4, meeting 3 May 1819.

79 RCSI/COL/4, meeting 3 November 1823.

80 The building was destroyed by fire in 1916.

81 Bernadette Goslin, 'A history and descriptive catalogue of the Murray Collection of architectural drawings', unpublished MA thesis, University College Dublin 1990 p 239. Cameron, p 151.

82 Johnston also, however, 'recommended the consideration of Mr Carolan's plan and estimate' to the building committee. This was the architect Robinson Carolin, a member of the building firm and timber merchants of that name in Lower Abbey Street Dublin. Edward Carolin was the builder engaged by Johnston for the Royal Hibernian Academy on Abbey Street Dublin (1824–6) built to Johnston's design and his own expense. The Carolin firm also tendered for the building of the extension to the RCSI. www.dia.ie. On completion of the museum (and the extension) in 1827, a resolution was passed at a meeting on 7 July thanking Johnston 'for his polite attention and gratuitous assistance to the Museum Building Committee on all occasions during the progress of the present building', RCSI/COL/5, meeting 7 July 1827.

83 Quote from Edward McParland in Bernadette Goslin, 'A history and descriptive catalogue of the Murray Collection of architectural drawings', unpublished MA thesis, University College Dublin, 1990.

84 RCSI/COL/5, meeting 27 July 1925. The other firms who tendered were Williams & Cockburn (£6320), Edward Carolin & Co. (£5700) and James & Patrick Whelan (£5370).

85 Brennan, 'The Royal College of Surgeons in Ireland' p 18.

86 Attached to this plan is a flap giving a very plain, and obviously much cheaper, alternative for the extension.

87 RCSI Archives, BF LO/An/30(3), Letter 28 April 1825 from Murray to the RCSI.

88 RCSI/MUC/1, Minutes of Museum Building Committee 9 March 1825–16 November 1840, meeting 24 September 1825.

89 RCSI/MUC/1 meeting 3 November 1825.

OPENING OF THE ROYAL COLLEGE OF SURGEONS IN IRELAND-
MEDICAL UNIVERSITY OF BAHRAIN 3 FEBRUARY 2009

Plate X: Official opening by the President of Ireland, Mary McAleese, in the presence of His Highness Shaikh Khalifa bin Salman Al Khalifa, Prime Minister of the Kingdom of Bahrain, 3 February, 2009

Plate XI: The Atrium

OPENING OF THE ROYAL COLLEGE OF SURGEONS IN IRELAND- MEDICAL UNIVERSITY OF BAHRAIN 3 FEBRUARY 2009

Plate XII: View from the southwest, with the Sheik Isa Bin Salman Causeway

Plate XIII: Dry stone walling

90 Alan Browne and Beatrice Doran, 'The external statuary of the Royal College of Surgeons in Ireland' in *Journal of the Irish Colleges of Physicians and Surgeons,* vol. 17, No. 4, October 1988, pp 177–9. John Smyth was responsible for the heads of Palladio, Michelangelo and Raphael over the doors and windows at the RHA building in Abbey Street, Dublin.

91 There are two drawings of this in the College collection, one dated 4 October 1825, the other 7 February 1826.

92 Carlisle Bridge was rebuilt in 1876, removing the 'hump' in the centre, and widening it substantially.

93 RCSI/COL/5, meeting 17 March 1827.

94 RCSI/MUC/1, meetings 20 June and 5 July 1827.

95 As built, the library extension to the front of the building was not executed and, in an 1875 plan, the old entrance hall is annotated 'vestibule', and the three rooms on its left converted into a single space, called 'Fellows room'.

96 RCSI Archives, LO An 30/1/(11) letter from Murray 25 May 1827. The extra cost of this he estimated at £155.6s.1d.

97 In conversation with the author 7 June 2009.

98 RCSI/COL/5, meeting 13 June 1827.

99 RCSI/COL/5, meeting 23 December 1826, letter from William Murray from Architects Office, Dublin Castle, 11 December 1826; RCSI/MUC/1, meeting 28 December 1826.

100 RCSI Archives, LO AN 30/1/(3), letter from Murray 28 April 1825.

101 RCSI Archives, Box 3, No. 5, letter from William Murray from Architect's Office, Dublin Castle dated 13 November 1830.

102 Cameron, *History* p 269.

103 Parke's façade was not cut back: the junction between his and Millar & Symes' building is between the fifth and sixth bays from St Stephen's Green. Brennan 'The Royal College of Surgeons in Ireland' p 26.

104 The space beyond the columns (part of the old library) is called 'Dr Jacob's library' on Millar & Symes' plan.

105 Brennan 'The Royal College of Surgeons in Ireland' p 26.

106 Ibid., pp 40–1.

The College buildings in context

Christopher Moore

The building of the RCSI between 1805 and 1827 occurred at a defining moment for Dublin and Ireland. This period was one of change from the predominantly aristocratic patronage of the eighteenth century, to a more complicated era where democracy, mechanics and the middle classes played a larger role. With the passing of the Act of Union in 1800, Ireland lost its political independence, Dublin its political elite and economic recession for a time caused a hiatus in domestic building activity. Public building did recommence in the aftermath of the Act of Union but it was less conspicuous and often more utilitarian than that conceived in the previous century.[1]

Stylistic background and influences

Public buildings are important advertisements for the institutions they house. In the uncertain years of the early 1800s the importance of stylistic association in Ireland was not to be underestimated—in the case of the College the building marked the status and growing importance of the surgical profession, not all that long released from an association with apothecaries, barbers and wigmakers. The dignified Roman classicism of the College façade, although the product of an extended building programme, is stylistically comfortable with its Irish contemporaries and yet acknowledges more illustrious architectural predecessors. This second phase of construction has been criticised by Maurice Craig as having 'deprived it of most of its character',[2] however the noble pediment, balustrades, giant order, *piano nobile* and rustication, represent a version and a reminder of the great buildings of the Neo-Palladian and later traditions so successfully introduced to Ireland in the years after 1715.

Economic stability in the second half of the eighteenth century had led to unprecedented development in the arts of architecture and decoration in Ireland and emulation of these in the early years of the nineteenth century demonstrated confident resolve. Under the Hanoverian kings, politics was dominated by the Whig party whose rationalism led to the adoption of the Palladian architectural and decorative style, epitomised by the Parliament House in Dublin's College Green. On the grounds of purity, clarity and practicality they promoted ancient classical architecture translated through the work of the Italian High Renaissance architect, Andrea Palladio (1508–80) and his contemporaries—referred to subsequently as Neo-Palladianism.

It was a dogged, masculine, confident style that appealed to the entrepreneurs of both the eighteenth and the early nineteenth centuries. The component parts of Palladian buildings were clearly identifiable, grandeur was the keynote but the lucidity of Palladian architecture meant that within them everyone knew their place and there was a natural progression from noble exterior, through a columnar hall, to an ascent via triumphal staircase to a grand first floor saloon. Even in the early nineteenth century this had a colonial appropriateness in Ireland.

Although the staid and proper Palladio-inspired architecture of the early to mid eighteenth century remained a dominant force, elements of it began to dissolve between 1750 and 1770. The second generation of Neo-Palladians reacted against the earlier formality, developing an ever increasing interest in decorative frivolity. The scented, decorative and informal manners of Paris and Madame de Pompadour spread across the British Isles and broke down the constraints of polite society. In Ireland this found a ready home. Freeing itself from conventions, this French inspired Rococo style found inspiration in things natural and exotic—bouquets, shells and things oriental. Wealth and prosperity were celebrated as never before with rooms decked out with stucco bunting, gilded bouquets and a permanently festive spirit. In the context of the College it is somewhat surprising, but perhaps appropriate, that this vivid period of Irish productivity is represented by the fine mid-eighteenth century Rococo ceiling installed in the Colles Room in the late 1970s, having been saved from the demolished 15 South Frederick Street, Dublin. Executed in low relief, it is composed of free designs of swirling acanthus leaves, bouquets of flowers and cornucopia. It was a short lived style, but the Rococo was symptomatic of great changes. Its spontaneity and naturalism were in tune with the Enlightenment, the aesthetics of

Edmund Burke and the spirit of enquiry that lay behind the establishment of the College.

The College buildings also reflect the last phase of eighteenth century architectural inspiration—that of Neo-Classicism. Driven by a renewal of interest in the study of antiquity, this later eighteenth century style represented a more profound study of architecture and the origins of civilisation. Husks, sphinxes, and ornament drawn from the excavations at Herculaneum and Pompeii replaced both the robust Renaissance inspired mouldings of the Neo-Palladians and the naturalism of the Rococo. Archaeological discoveries were refined and made delicate for sensibilities fed by the theories of Edmund Burke's concept of Beauty. Echoes of this Enlightenment revival of antiquity are found in Edward Parke's ox head Entrance Hall frieze in the College and in the ceiling of the Board Room. The establishment of the College in 1784 was very much part of the Enlightenment project, which increased interest in, and understanding of, the sciences in the late eighteenth century. The College wanted to reflect the discoveries of the old century and the aspirations of the new.

So the College buildings, as erected in two phases, 1806–10 and 1825–7, represent a summation of a century of Irish eighteenth century architectural developments. Parke's original pedimented building has been likened to a simple classical church in the tradition well established in Dublin during the eighteenth century, though more austere and antique.[3] A close precedent might be found in the former Free Church, Great Charles Street, off Mountjoy Square (Fig. 1) built in 1800 and designed by Edward Robbins, its podium, arched recess, window and blind panels on the *piano nobile* have an air of simple but grand austerity akin to Parke's College building.[4]

Parke and Murray's completed building is perhaps closer to the New Assembly Rooms, Cavendish Row, (Fig. 2) begun in 1784 by Murray's kinsman Richard Johnston, with its *piano nobile*, pedimented centre-piece and terminating paired order sitting on a rusticated projecting base. In the College, the combination of Wicklow granite for the bulk of the façade with the highlighting of the Tuscan border, entablature, balustrades and sculpture in Portland stone follows the eighteenth century tradition of many Dublin public buildings. The ornamentation of the pediment by John Smyth is in the tradition of his father Edward's famous sculptural works for James Gandon at the Custom House, Four Courts and the King's Inns. Just as in Gandon's buildings, the sculptural iconography underlines the nature of the building it adorns. It reflects loyalty to the Crown, and also the serious intent behind the establishment of the College as a professional body representing the scientific and other interests of surgeons.

Fig. 1: Free Church, Great Charles Street, Dublin, 1800, Edward Robbins (Courtesy Irish Architectural Archive, photo, Peter Costello)

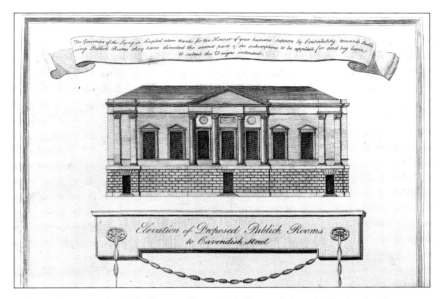

Fig. 2: Proposed Public Rooms, Cavendish Row, Dublin by Richard Johnston, c. 1784 (Courtesy Irish Architectural Archive, original in the collection of the Rotunda Hospital)

The Regency context

The Regency period (c. 1790–1837), during which the greater part of the College was built, was one of great social and political change. In addition to Ireland's particular situation, the American War of Independence, the French Revolution and the developing Industrial Revolution all impacted on the nature of society throughout Europe. Between 1793 and 1815, bar brief respites, England was at war with France. As Patricia McCarthy describes, money was tight, taxes were high and civic architecture was curtailed. At the same time, because of the war, there was a brisk demand for surgeons for the army and navy. This had previously been acknowledged by the then Lord Lieutenant who, in 1784, had referred to the urgent need 'to establish a liberal and extensive system of surgical education in Ireland'.[5] George Renny, Director General of the Army Medical Department, astute businessman and key member of the College, was well positioned to see that the College was a beneficiary of the funding that the government invested in institutions that trained and produced medical men.

After the Battle of Waterloo there was in England a return to the entrepreneurial world of private enterprise, speculative development and the public building of hospitals, museums, schools and a myriad of churches financed by the Church Building Act of 1818—the 'Million Pounds Act'—all of which changed the face of London.[6] Dublin was little different—the upheavals in Europe, the social and political changes following 1798 and the Act of Union led to the gradual replacement of the old hierarchy by a growing professional class whose presence led to the expansion of the city and the establishment of the suburbs. Maurice Craig has referred to the lawyers, clerics and doctors who made up the cream of early nineteenth century Dublin society.

This replacement of the old order by the professions undoubtedly accounts for the conservatism exhibited in much of Irish Regency domestic architecture—notably the Pembroke Estate where the nineteenth century houses of Fitzwilliam Square are more modest echoes of their eighteenth century predecessors in Merrion Square. Perhaps the same can be said for the design for the College buildings. In London and Edinburgh, the sister colleges were being built at almost

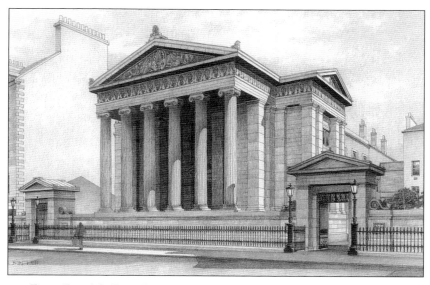

Fig. 3: Royal College of Surgeons, College Hall, Nicolson Street, Edinburgh, architect William Playfair, 1830–32
(Courtesy the Royal College of Surgeons, Edinburgh)

the same time, using well-known architects who produced buildings representing the very latest Greek revival version of Neo-Classicism (Fig. 3). In conservative Dublin, not unaware of European trends but perhaps a little insecure, George Renny and his committee chose Edward Parke, and later William Murray, as their architects. These men were well schooled and competent and the extended building programme produced a structure that could not be described as *avant-garde* but nevertheless reflected the dignity and serious purpose of their clients and enhanced the prestige of the College.[7]

Apart from occasional forays into Gothic or Egyptian styles, British Regency architecture of the period developed the Neo-Classical revival with an emphasis on the more archaic architecture of ancient Greece. There was in effect a shift from Edmund Burke's concept of delicate Beauty, which had been pursued in the late eighteenth century, to an espousal of the Sublime which was dependent on scale, drama and was intended to inspire awe. The creation of such buildings was fuelled by the increasing popularity of primitive architecture. As noted, the comparable Colleges in London and Edinburgh chose this style for their new buildings.[8] The medical profession was still conscious of its classical inheritance, and in the early nineteenth century students entering the College had to pass examinations in Latin and Greek and be familiar with Virgil, Horace and Homer.[9] This style, '*le gout Grec*' as it was known was especially popular during and just after the Napoleonic wars and, with its austere air of grandeur, seemed an appropriate style for public building. Its vogue lasted until the 1830s, after which the future lay with the Gothic revival.

Dublin benefited from the work of two key English Greek Revivalists: William Wilkins, who produced the original designs for Nelson's Pillar in 1808 (Fig. 4) in what was then Sackville Street, and Sir Robert Smirke, whose Wellington Monument in the Phoenix Park was started in 1817 (Fig. 5). These structures, and St Mary's Pro-Cathedral of *c.* 1825 (Fig. 6),[10] follow this new philosophy and look for inspiration from the early civilisations of the Mediterranean. Ireland had finally come to terms with the architecture of Greece. The Pro-Cathedral, although awkwardly sited, powerfully recalls the fifth century BC Theseion in Athens, with an interior adapted to Christian liturgy and a baseless Doric

[75]

order continuing into an apse. Other less extreme examples include the Greek Ionic St Stephen's Mount Street of 1821 by John Bowden (Fig. 7) and the Greek Doric St Andrew's Westland Row by James Bolger of 1837 (Fig. 8). Francis Johnston, who inherited the mantle of principal public architect from James Gandon, was a practitioner of this sublime style as best seen in a public building in the GPO, O'Connell Street, (1814–18) (Fig. 4). Despite the fact that the Greek Revival had become the most appropriate style for public buildings by the time the College was looking at expanding, perhaps this 'certain hardness (that) distinguishes nearly all his work'[11] made Johnston too austere a choice. McCarthy has noted that, in any case, Johnston was ill and at the end of his career in the mid 1820s: recommending his able but less talented assistant was undoubtedly a safe alternative.

Fig. 4: Nelson's Pillar, O'Connell Street, Dublin. William Wilkins and Francis Johnston 1808. General Post Office: Francis Johnston 1814–18. (Courtesy the National Library of Ireland)

THE COLLEGE BUILDINGS IN CONTEXT

*Fig. 5: Wellington Monument, Phoenix Park, Dublin, 1817–61, Sir Robert Smirke
(Courtesy the National Library of Ireland)*

*Fig. 6: The Pro Cathedral, Dublin: c. 1825
(Courtesy the National Library of Ireland)*

[77]

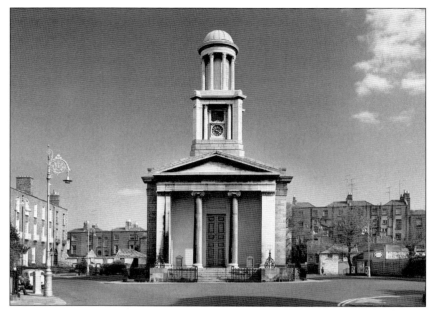

*Fig. 7: St Stephen's Church, Mount Street, Dublin, 1821, John Bowden
(Courtesy Davison & Associates)*

*Fig. 8: St Andrew's Church, Westland Row, Dublin, 1837, James Bolger
(Courtesy Davison & Associates)*

THE COLLEGE BUILDINGS IN CONTEXT

The classicism of the College buildings

Patricia McCarthy has outlined the probable reasons behind the choice of Edward Parke as architect in 1805—notably his acquaintance with, and patronage from, Speaker Foster and his prestigious position as architect for the Commercial Buildings, the Linen Board and the extension to the House of Commons. Although not seen today as being of the calibre of Francis Johnston, Parke was clearly well regarded as an establishment figure at the turn of the eighteenth century, capable of producing designs that reflected existing Dublin buildings and yet also being at least partially responsible for the memorably severe and *avant-garde* Greek Revival Dundalk Court House in 1813. Perhaps it is significant that James Gandon, who represented the old Neo-Palladian tradition of Lord Charlemont, Sir William Chambers and eighteenth century sensibilities, retired in 1808 during which time Parke's College building was being erected. With Gandon out of the way, Francis Johnston, his replacement at the Board of Works, was free to become Ireland's most adventurous Greek Revival architect.[12] This enabled less experienced architects, like Parke, to explore current European architectural trends. The original College building marks a transition from his acknowledgement of the old Palladian order to his brilliant embracement of the revival of the primitive.

Parke's College building is unmistakably of its era. Despite its eighteenth century patrimony it could not be mistaken for one of its predecessors. The very choice of the Tuscan order for the facade, although Roman, is primitive and is a nod towards the then current interest in the origins of architecture. There is an overall coarseness of detail and heaviness in handling of the building that is part of this aesthetic and differentiates it from the elegance or grandeur of many eighteenth century public buildings. Indeed in the George Petrie illustration of Parke's building there is a certain grandeur, reminiscent of ancient Rome, with its Tuscan portico and side elevation patterned with blind windows, lunettes and alternating semi-circular and rectangular frames. Parke's concept of an unornamented temple on a podium, articulated by a certain play of light and shade with its deeply channelled joints indicating sobriety and weight, are all appropriate to the creation of 'a dignified national temple dedicated to surgical science'.[13]

[79]

With the help of Murray's later drawings and the surviving spaces it is still possible to experience Parke's intended Neo-Classical drama. Visitors passed through the long dark entrance hall and were drawn to the top-lit staircase which, by contrast, was flooded with light from the domes above. This staircase was dramatic with its turned, shallow, Portland steps and wrought iron rail, rising in three simple flights to the first floor lobby, lit by the dome itself springing from elegant pendentives. This is an attempt to create a true Neo-Classical experience with the raking light defining and modelling the architectural forms and creating a *chiaroscuro* reminiscent of Piranesi's visions of Rome. Francis Johnston successfully achieved this theatrical combination of the beautiful and the sublime in the extraordinary and near contemporary top-lit stairhall in Townley Hall, Co. Louth. This use of top-lighting and simplified yet powerful architectural forms was perhaps most famously used to dramatic effect by Sir John Soane in his designs for the Bank of England dating from the late 1790s. Some years after the College buildings, Parke developed further his handling of space at the Dundalk Court House—itself an essay in Greek Doric severity drawn straight from the pages of James 'Athenian' Stuart's *Antiquities of Athens*.[14] There, the plan is remarkable with a processional axis through the building to the rere and a sensational bifurcating top-lit staircase (Fig 9).

At the College, the drama continued into the upper lobby, the dome of which very probably retains its original decoration: this acted as a vestibule either to the now lost Museum or the Board Room overlooking St Stephen's Green. The theme of the staircase was evidently continued in the Museum which though rather narrow, was of double height, barrel vaulted with coffers and lit by four, high, Roman Diocletian windows.

The Board Room, which survives largely intact, derives from the tradition of grand first floor saloons so well represented in eighteenth century Dublin houses. Replacing the Palladian Baroque or Rococo decoration of the mid eighteenth century, here there is a shallow barrel vault with three compartments decorated with arabesque motifs. Inspiration for this room lies in grand Dublin Neo-Classical interiors like the 1780 shallow vaulted Library (now Seanad Chamber) in Leinster House, designed by James Wyatt, or even Gandon's Dining Hall in King's Inns of 1800. What has changed, though, is that the decoration is coarser and

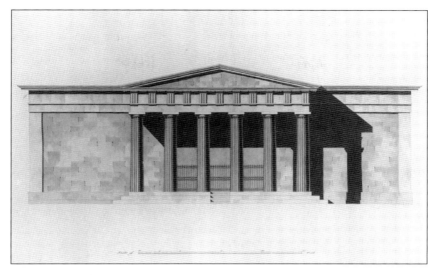

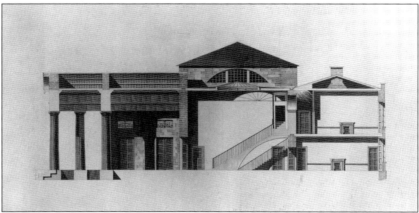

*Fig. 9 (a+b) Dundalk Court House, Dundalk, Co. Louth, 1813, Edward Parke and others, elevation and transverse drawing by Owen Fahy, original in the collection of Dundalk County Museum
(Courtesy the Irish Architectural Archive)*

the mouldings heavier, but this is in keeping with decorative tendencies as they developed in the years around the turn of the nineteenth century. It is interesting that in 1825, William Murray respected Parke's work and warned the College officers against damaging 'the handsome coved ceiling' of the Board Room.[15] Murray's regard for the by then rather old-fashioned decoration of Parke's room is indicative of his continuing respect for the eighteenth century. Even by Dublin's conservative standards, the room must have seemed outdated by the 1820s. Around the corner in the Carmelite Church, Whitefriar St, in 1825–7 George Papworth designed a similar shallow vaulted space which was less pretty and more austere with simply decorated coffers replacing the elaborate arabesque decoration seen in the College (Fig. 10). If the Board Room ceiling looks back to the eighteenth century, the twin chimneypieces give a hint of Edward Parke's future, austere Grecian style. Recently cleaned of their gloss paint, they are made of Kilkenny limestone and are designed with minimal decoration and a linear simplicity—they are in fact close to published designs by the aesthete and art collector, Thomas Hope.[16]

Fig. 10: The Carmelite Church, Dublin reproduced from the Dublin Penny Journal, *7 October 1832 (Courtesy the Irish Architectural Archive)*

The number of students continued to grow in the second decade of the nineteenth century[17] and so the College had to expand. In 1825, William Murray was appointed to alter and extend the original building. Murray's drawings for the proposed works are typical of the period—clear, handsome, colour-coded documents which acted both as axiomatic presentation drawings and working documents for the contractors. Although Francis Johnston's assistant, Murray was hardly

Plate XIV: State Corridor in Dublin Castle, Thomas Eyre, Dublin, c. 1758

Plate XV: Borromini Corridor at the Spada Palace, Francesco Borromini, Rome, 1635

his equal, and even allowing for the difficulties of re-using materials and adapting Parke's building, the result moves away from the austere Greek Revival to a tamer Renaissance-inspired classicism. Although he subsequently had a prominent career in the Board of Works, Murray's houses and public buildings, built for example in Armagh city in the 1830s, are Palladian, conservative and look firmly back to the genteel eighteenth century tradition introduced by Thomas Cooley in the 1770s. It is small wonder that, as McCarthy points out, the new entrance hall of 1827 possibly draws inspiration from Richard Castle's Rotunda Hospital (Fig. 11) of the 1750s, although the wall and ceiling mouldings are in the spirit of Francis Johnston's St George's, Hardwick Place, of 1802–13. The new Museum room was more dramatic and might be compared to the King's Inns Library designed by Frederick Darley at the same time (Fig. 12). Both long, rectangular spaces had Doric pilasters supporting a gallery, though in the College Murray introduced an upper Ionic order above which were the four domes. Darley's library survives intact and has a heavy monumental clarity. Had Murray's Museum not been radically altered in 1905, it would be less severe, but nonetheless noble and very possibly the architectural highlight of the College.

Fig. 11: The Rotunda Hospital, Parnell Street, Dublin, 1751, Richard Castle, entrance hall (Courtesy Davison & Associates)

SURGEONS' HALLS

Fig. 12: The King's Inns Library Henrietta Street, Dublin, 1826–30, Frederick Darley (Courtesy Davison & Associates)

The College art collection

The College maintained a high public profile—the building was positioned on an important thoroughfare. The foundation stones in both 1806 and 1825 were laid by the current Lord Lieutenant and the original Charter and the Supplemental Charter were granted by the reigning monarchs.[18] This royal association was confirmed by key elements in the College art collection. There is a fine bust of George III by Edward and John Smyth of *c.* 1809 (Fig. 13) and a noble portrait bust of George IV in Field Marshal's uniform of 1823 (Fig. 14)[19]. The College desired a portrait of the monarch because, according to the then President, Charles Hawkes Todd, the sovereign 'has raised the medical profession in the three Kingdoms to a rank above that which it holds in any other country'.[20]

Fig. 13: Bust of George III by Edward and John Smyth, c. 1809 (Courtesy Davison & Associates)

Fig. 14: Bust of George IV, unattributed, 1823 (Courtesy Davison & Associates)

The College has always had a strong sense of history and tradition, almost continuously commissioning and acquiring a portrait and statuary collection that underpins and enriches these values. During the nineteenth century, other institutions such as the King's Inns and Bank of Ireland did likewise, though the latter's commissioning of works by Thomas Lawrence, John Bacon and Peter Turnerelli was in a different league to that of the College. Nevertheless, the collection is significant. There are at least 50 painted portraits and 34 portrait busts. The sculpture collection has representative works by most of the leading sculptors working in Ireland in the nineteenth and early twentieth centuries: John and Edward Smyth, Christopher Moore, Thomas Kirk, Sir Thomas Farrell, John Henry Foley and John Henry Sheppard. Apart from the two monarchs, there is a bust by Thomas Kirk of Hugh Percy, third Duke of Northumberland, who as Lord Lieutenant of Ireland (1829–30) donated £500 to the College for the purchase of anatomical preparations in wax.[21] The remaining collection of sculpture of professionals

*Fig. 15: Bust of John Kirby by Thomas Kirk, 1833
(Courtesy Davison & Associates)*

and College officers adds gravitas to their classical setting. Amongst the most sensitive are John Smyth's posthumous 1812 bust of William Dease, a founding member of the College. More vigorous, but equally humane, is the 1833 bust of John Kirby by Thomas Kirk (Fig. 15). From 1810 until 1860, the College commissioned sculpture at regular intervals as a mark of respect for members or staff. Since that time, any that the

Fig. 16: Statue of William Dease by Sir Thomas Farrell, 1886 (Courtesy Davison & Associates)

SURGEONS' HALLS

College has acquired have been presented by individuals or memorial committees.[22] One of the most dramatic of these is the life-size, seated figure of William Dease by Sir Thomas Farrell of 1886. Executed nearly 100 years after his death, this informally dressed, but imposing, figure dominates the Entrance Hall (Fig. 16)

Members of the medical profession were amongst the earliest professionals to have themselves recorded in portraits.[23] Some of the painted portraits might be described as conventional, but cumulatively they are an interesting record of upper-middle-class Irish society. Two of the most dramatic early portraits are huge canvases: that of James Henthorn by Martin Cregan, 1826 and George Renny by William Cuming, 1810. These rather heroic canvases of key early members of the College depict

Fig. 17: Portrait of Oliver St John Gogarty by Sir William Orpen, 1911, oil on canvas (Courtesy Davison & Associates)

[90]

the larger than life-size subjects from below, are identically framed and dominate the Board Room. More intimate and humane are the portraits of Abraham Colles by Martin Cregan (1837) and Thomas Lewis Mackesy by Stephen Catterson Smith (1864). While many of the pictures are conventional academic depictions of Victorian professionals, there are some fine early twentieth century portraits. Notable amongst these is a fine Sir William Orpen of Oliver St John Gogarty (1911), (Fig. 17) a Leo Whelan of Sir Thomas Myles and a Harry Kernoff of Tom Garry. The tradition continues and in recent years Presidents of the College have been painted by Thomas Ryan, Carey Clarke, James Hart Dyke and James Hanley.

Later building developments

Throughout the nineteenth century the College expanded, receiving its Supplemental Charter in 1844 from Queen Victoria, creating a chair of Dental Surgery in 1884, incorporating the private Carmichael and Ledwich schools in 1889 and at the same time adding new chairs of Pathology and Biology. As the departments and student numbers grew, pressure was brought to bear on the original site and alterations and additions were carried out that inevitably compromised the Regency building. Some of the alterations carried out by Millar and Symes between 1875 and 1878 were sympathetic, particularly the extension of Parke's original York Street façade. High Victorian architecture was eclectic and the surprise appearance of the pillared opening in the stairhall designed in the Venetian Gothic manner reflects the then current stylistic upheavels in the British Isles. This style had been promoted by John Ruskin from 1850 because it represented truthfulness and individuality. Deane and Woodward's Museum Building in Trinity College of 1853–7 perfectly embodied this reaction to mainstream Victorian architecture. The incongruity of this stylistic intervention in an otherwise classical teaching establishment must reflect a topical acceptance on the part of the College of Ruskin's arguments in *The Seven Lamps of Architecture* (1849) and *The Stones of Venice* (1851–3) where he invoked morality in the suitability of architectural styles.

By the mid twentieth century the original site was inadequate for the College. From 1953 it gradually acquired additional property—mainly adjoining old houses which had gradually declined from their eighteenth century grandeur into tenements. A fundraising programme in the late 1970s resulted in the construction of a new Medical School designed by Frank Foley of Buchan, Kane and Foley—a huge structure faced in precast concrete panels framing large windows with rounded reveals and a link building built in 1978. The uncompromising modernism of the new buildings reflected the growing international stature of the College, a feature noted in 1978 by the then President, Stanley McCollum, who recorded that the College was training 700 students, three-quarters of whom came from 35 other countries.[24]

A programme of restoration of the historically significant portions of the College was initiated in the late 1970s. In 1977 the Albert Theatre was reinstated, between 1978 and 1981 the Colles Room ceiling and a fine chimneypiece were introduced[25] and in 1980/1 Parke and Murray's St Stephen's Green facade was extensively cleaned and restored.[26] Over the past decade, the principal rooms in the old College have been redecorated in an attempt to make them less institutional and more historically sympathetic. Most recently, a room off the College Hall, for many years used as a servery, has been successfully refitted as a Council Room to designs by Sheehan and Barry Architects. The College Hall itself was redecorated in 2010. Architecturally it is now a curious amalgam of Murray's four domes and opulent Edwardian mahogany fittings. The overall colour scheme has been toned down, gilding introduced into the domes and the giant Ionic pilasters marbled in a green Brocatelle to give strength and visual cohesion to the room.

Bahrain

The cultural fusion which has enriched both the College and Dublin City is reflected in the new Medical University of Bahrain. There is a curious circumstantial similarity between the early years of the College in leased buildings in Mercer Street and the rented accommodation in the Seef district in Manama. Just as the College acquired its prominent position on St Stephen's Green in 1805, the building of the new campus in the Busaiteen area on Muharraq Island in 2006 placed the new College near a major thoroughfare that called for a prominent building. Parke and Murray looked to the ancient world for inspiration, so too did

THE COLLEGE BUILDINGS IN CONTEXT

the Aedas design team with their use of Bahraini and Irish Neolithic cultural symbols. Just as the 1810–25 building both reflected and influenced the course of the College's fortunes through the nineteenth and twentieth centuries, the new Bahrain building is a landmark structure for the Royal College of Surgeons in Ireland in the twenty-first century.

Acknowledgements

I would like to thank Patricia McCarthy, David Griffin, the staff of the Irish Architectural Archive and Prof. Clive Lee for their help and advice in the preparation of this chapter.

Notes

1   Christine Casey, *The Buildings of Ireland: Dublin* (New Haven and London 2005) p 51.
2   Maurice James Craig, *Dublin 1660–1860* (London 1952) p 280.
3   Casey, *The Buildings of Ireland: Dublin* p 484.
4   The author is grateful to Peter Costello for permission to reproduce this image which first appeared in his book *Dublin Churches* (Dublin 1989).
5   Quoted in Colin Brennan, 'The Royal College of Surgeons in Ireland: an architectural history 1805–1997', unpublished MA thesis, University College, Dublin 1997 p 6.
6   Giles Worsley, *Architectural Drawings of the Regency Period 1790–1837* (London 1991) p 1.
7   Brennan, 'The Royal College of Surgeons in Ireland' p 8.
8   Helen M. Dingwall, '*A Famous and Flourishing Society*', *The History of the Royal College of Surgeons of Edinburgh, 1505–2000 (*Edinburgh 2005). pp 274, 275. On page 155 she notes the close links between the Dublin and Edinburgh colleges.
9   Louise Masterson, 'A Catalogue of the Collection of Painted and Sculpted Portraits in the Royal College of Surgeons in Ireland' Vols 1 and 2. unpublished thesis 1991, p 24.
10 Michael McCarthy, *Classical and Gothic, Studies in History of Art* (Dublin 2005) p 66.
11 Craig *Dublin 1660–1860* p 281.
12 Michael McCarthy, *Classical and Gothic* p 72.
13 Brennan 'The Royal College of Surgeons in Ireland', p 9.
14 McCarthy, *Classical and Gothic* p 75.
15 Brennan, 'The Royal College of Surgeons in Ireland' p 10.
16 Illustrated in Thomas Hope, *Household Furniture and Interior Decoration,* (New York 1971) pl xxv.
17 Brennan, 'The Royal College of Surgeons in Ireland', p 6.

[93]

SURGEONS' HALLS

18 J. D. H. Widdess, *The Royal College of Surgeons in Ireland and its Medical School 1784–1984* (Dublin 1984 ed.), p 63 the Lord Lieutenant, the Duke of Bedford laid the foundation stone on 17 March 1806; p 68 the Marquess of Wellesley laid the foundation stone of the Murray building on 21 September 1825. Queen Victoria granted the Supplemental Charter in 1844 pp 90–2.

19 Masterson, 'A Catalogue' pp 87, 88, this is on loan from the National Gallery of Ireland who acquired it between 1890–8.

20 Ibid., p 89: as quoted from the College Minutes of 25 August 1821.

21 Ibid., p 143.

22 Ibid., p 18.

23 Ibid., p 4 quoted from O'Brien E., Crookshank A., Wolstenholme G., *A Portrait of Irish Medicine: An Illustrated History of Medicine in Ireland* (Dublin 1984).

24 Widdess, *The Royal College of Surgeons in Ireland* p 131.

25 Brennan, 'The Royal College of Surgeons in Ireland' p 49.

26 Widdess, *The Royal College of Surgeons in Ireland* p 132.

THE WIDDESS LECTURE

John David Henry Widdess (1906–82), known as Jack, was born in Limerick and educated at Wesley College Dublin, the Royal College of Surgeons in Ireland and Trinity College Dublin. A medical doctor, natural scientist and Doctor of Letters, he served RCSI from 1931 as physiologist, biochemist, pathologist, librarian, journal editor and ultimately as Professor of Biology from 1960 until his retirement in 1973.

On his appointment in 1931, he was instrumental in the revival of the student Biological Society and thereafter never missed an inaugural meeting.[1] As its permanent Vice-President and President, and as President of the Literary and Dramatic Society, he encouraged the intellectual and artistic life of the College and began each academic year with a talk on its history. In 1941 he became the College's librarian, reorganising its collections, both modern and historical. From the time of his book *An Account of the Schools of Surgery, Royal College of Surgeons, Dublin 1789–1948* (first edition 1949) he became recognised as Ireland's premier medical historian, publishing numerous books and papers on the subject. In 1968 he was elected an honorary fellow of the RCPI.

In 1977, the Biological Society instituted the J. D. H. Widdess Lecture in his honour, with the first delivered by J. B. Lyons.[2] In recent years, this tradition has lapsed.

To celebrate 200 years of the College on St Stephen's Green, it was agreed that the Widdess Lecture be established as an occasional College Lecture on an artistic theme.

Clive Lee

---

1 H. Andrews, 'Widdess, J. D. H.' in *Dictionary of Irish Biography from the earliest times to the year 2002* (Cambridge, 2009) pp 923–5.

2 J. B. Lyons, 'The Hall of Fame' in *Journal of the Irish College of Physicians and Surgeons* vol 71, 1978, p 237

The 2010 Widdess Lecture
Corridic modernities—
space and interiority in nineteenth-
& twentieth-century architecture

Mark Jarzombek

Foreword

The gradual emergence in the late eighteenth and early nineteenth centuries of post-Enlightenment society changed the architectural landscape of our cities. Parliament buildings and state houses, as well as buildings for law courts, ministries and professional societies, along with those for universities, stores, and offices all became part of a new architectural 'package'. Typically we have looked at these buildings from the outside and discussed them in terms of style and programme. But there is a significant common feature that most of these buildings came to share—a corridor. This spatial form is today so ubiquitous that one hardly thinks that it has a history. However, as the differences between the planning of the original building of the Royal College of Surgeons in Ireland (1810) and the recently-built building for the same institution in Bahrain indicate, the corridor only became a part of the 'package' relatively recently. Whereas the Bahrain building is designed around a grand curving corridor that links the building from end to end, the original building in Dublin had no corridor. It was created on the model of an Italian palazzo with a grand *piano nobile* (the Board Room) on the upper floor over-looking St Stephen's Green.

The Neo-Classical style with its columns, pilasters, rusticated stone-work and pediment spoke of the great ideals of the Renaissance and its ideology of historical continuity. But after the middle of the nineteenth century, a modern 'architecture of the institution' came into being, one in which continuity no longer needed to be emphasised. The professional class separated itself from the class of aristocratic gentlemen, and as a consequence, architecture loosened its grip on historicism to become more inventive. In this new world, the corridor became the symbol of a culture that prided itself on the principles (though not always the practices) of efficiency, objectivity and merit. The corridor was a new and different circulatory system both in the building and in society. One can think, in this respect, of the Victorian-era court houses, post offices, hospitals, and city halls with their great corridic interiors. This was in some sense more of a revolution of sensibilities than the advent of functionalist modernism in the 1920s and 30s.

There are many reasons to visit Dublin Castle, but for most visitors its State Corridor, built in 1758 to the designs of Thomas Eyre, is probably little more than a passing curiosity (Plate XIV, page 83).[1] Yet in its day, this space, with its vaulted and sky-lit ceilings—now altered after a restoration—and used as the ceremonial route for the Privy Councillors, was one of the most innovative and one can also say one of the most modern aspects of the building. Today, corridors are so ubiquitous in our public buildings that one can hardly imagine that they played anything other than a relatively trivial part in the history of architecture. But this is not the case.

The corridor, which entered architectural discourse only around the middle of the seventeenth century, rose to become the spatial element *par excellence* of modern civic architecture in the late nineteenth century. This significance is not much discussed in scholarship, where the corridor has been associated almost exclusively with the private sphere, leading some to lament its negative impact on our lives. Robin Evans, an English scholar writing in the 1970s, for example, argued that the corridor, with its machine-age linearity and isolated rooms, played a significant role in 'obliterating vast areas of social experience.'[2]

Tempting as it might be to explain the cause of our contemporary alienation in this way, the history of the corridor is far more complex than this critique suggests. In fact, the corridor through most of its history was less a private space than a type of public one. An English visitor to Germany in 1789, for example, noted with some astonishment that the Emperor, at five in the afternoon, goes 'to the Corridor just near his own apartment, where poor and rich, small and great, have access to his person at pleasure, and often get him to arbitrate their law-suits.'[3] Though the history of the corridor begins in the seventeenth century, it remained quite uncommon as an architectural element until the middle of the nineteenth century, which is why the Dublin Castle corridor is so remarkable. Soane's Bank of England (begun 1788) had no corridors and even the enormous Somerset House (1776–86), England's first large-scale government building, made only limited use of them. The architect of Somerset House, William Chambers, defines 'corridors' in his dictionary of architectural terms only as an element of domestic architecture, no doubt creating the illusion—and to some degree the error—that corridors are primarily a feature of private houses.[4] If corridors were being built in English-speaking countries in the late eighteenth century, they were in prisons, as in the formidable Kilmainham Gaol in Dublin (Plate XXI, page 120). But even in that context they were considered a novelty.

The rather hesitant use of corridors in English public architecture of the early nineteenth century was reinforced by their image as dark and lonely, sometimes even haunted. Charlotte Brontë visualised them as places for restless souls; Charles Robert Maturin in *Melmouth the Wanderer* (1820), made them into places of spectral encounter; for Byron they were convenient props for the Romantic soul. 'But glimmering through the dusky corridor,' he wrote in 1814 in *Corsair*, 'Another [lamp] chequers o'er the shadow'd floor.'[5] By 1877, however, when Henry James wrote *The American*, the perspective on the corridor had changed considerably. The main character of the book, the successful businessman, Christopher Newman,

> passed his arm into that of his companion, and the two walked for some time up and down one of the less frequented corridors. Newman's imagination began to glow with the idea of converting his bright, impracticable friend into a first-class man of business.[6]

The difference between the old and new is clearly manifest in the difference between the Royal Exchange in London (1844) and St George's Hall in Liverpool (1841–54) (Figs 1, 2). On the outside, both buildings, with their imposing, columnar porticoes, look equally classical. But their plans tell a different story. The former, in Georgian tradition, has no corridors whereas the latter is organised around a corridor system

CORRIDIC MODERNITIES

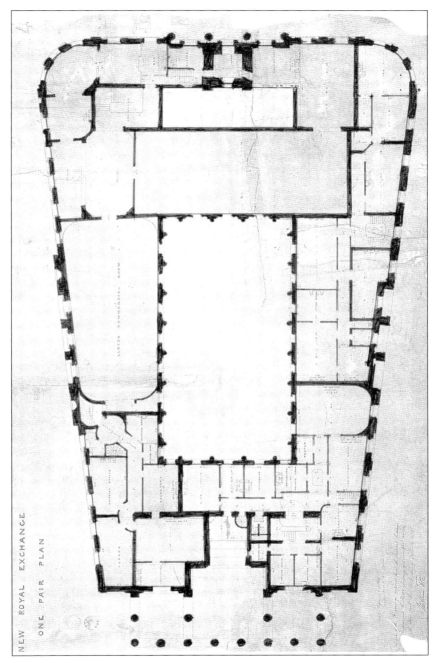

Fig. 1: Royal Exchange, William Tite, London, 1844

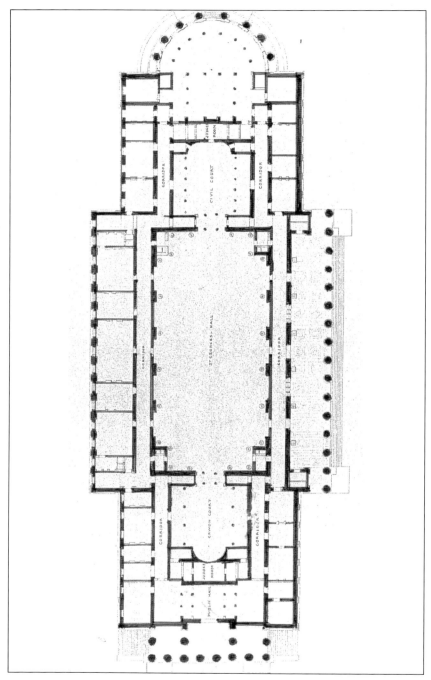

Fig. 2: St George's Hall, Harvey Lonsdale Elmes, Liverpool, 1841–54

Plate XVI: Vasari's Corridor, Giorgio Vasari, Florence, 1565

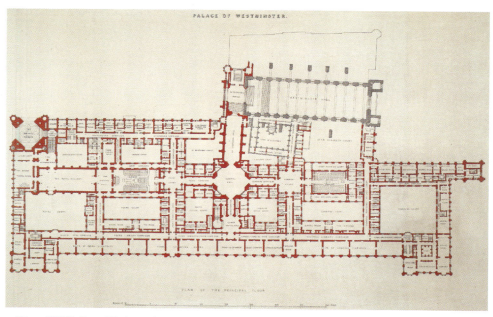

Plate XVII: Royal Palace of Westminster, Charles Barry and Augustus Welby Pugin, London, 1840–60

Plate XVIII: Massachusetts Institute of Technology, view of corridor, William Welles Bosworth, Cambridge, MA, 1916

Plate XIX: The Royal Courts of Justice, George Edmund Street, London, 1870, interior

along its entire 150 metre length. Though St George's Hall is almost always discussed as an example of the Neo-Grecian style, and was seen by Nikolaus Pevsner, the doyen of English architectural history, as the finest example of that style in the world, it should instead be celebrated as a fully modern building.[7] It was modern not because its corridors were 'functional.' Tall, airy and with marble floors, they constituted the organising structure of the plan. Compared to the haphazard arrangement of the spaces of the Royal Exchange where, for example, the window of the toilet faces out onto the grand entrance loggia, the plan of St George's Hall is methodical, clear and purposeful, organised in a way that was obviously a function of the rise of the professional class and the creation in the Victorian era of large national bureaucracies, law courts, and government ministries. But this is the end—or almost the end—of the story rather than its beginning.

The first corridors

In the fourteenth century, in both Spanish and Italian contexts, a *corridor* referred not to a space, but to a courier; someone who, as the word's Latin root suggests, could run fast. A *corridor* might have been a scout sent behind enemy lines, a government messenger, a carrier of money, or even a negotiator arranging mercantile deals and marriages.[8] He could also have served on the battlefield, sending reports between commanders and officers.[9] This was the meaning of the word as used by Dante in the line, 'Corridor vidi per la terra vostra':

> I have erewhile seen horsemen moving camp,
> Begin the storming, and their muster make,
> And sometimes starting off for their escape;
> Corridors have I seen upon your land,
> O Aretines, and foragers go forth,
> Tournaments stricken, and the joustings run
> [*Inferno*, Canto XXII, l. 1–6][10]

By the seventeenth century, because of the increasing dominance of French culture, the word had become obsolete and was gradually replaced by *courier*. But by then the imprint of the word corridor on architectural language had been irrevocably set, primarily as a military term referring to spaces in fortifications that enabled rapid communication with troops.[11] Giovanni Villani's treatise on the history of Florence, the *Cronica Universale* (1324), refers to such a *corridoio* on the city walls of Florence.[12] A *corridoio* could also serve as a secret way in and out of a castle or palace, such as the one that was built connecting the Vatican and Castello S. Angelo, which the Pope could use in times of trouble.[13] Equally famous is the *corridoio* in Florence (1565) built by the Medici to connect the Palazo Pitti on one side of the Arno with the Palazzo Vecchio on the other side; it was placed at the level of the upper floors so no one could see into it as it crossed over streets and along the Ponte Vecchio bridge (Plate XVI, page 101).[14] At its entrance, an ingeniously designed room with several fake doors was used to slow down anyone who might have gained surreptitious access. Similar *corridoios* were built in Parma (1550s), Vigevano (1490s) and Urbino (1490s) and other places.[15]

The point to take away from this is that corridors were not found *inside* palaces or villas. A palazzo was entered by means of an *andito*, which derives, of course, from the word *andare* 'to go' or 'to walk.' One would

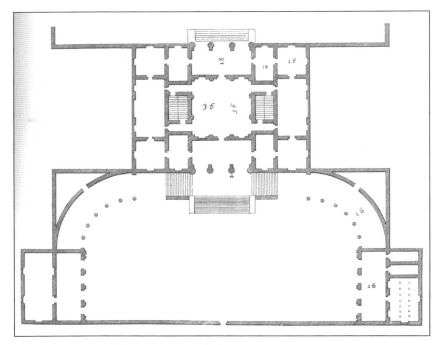

Fig. 3: Andrea Palladio, a villa design, 1560s

not have 'run' into a palazzo. The *andito* usually led to a *camminata*[16] (a 'walking place') or to a *passaggio*, which, if it was placed along a courtyard might have been called, from the fifteenth century onward, a *portico*, and sometimes a *loggia*. In Venice, the central hallway of a palace was known as a *portego*, which, like *portico*, comes from the Latin root *portare*. One was expected to 'carry oneself' with dignity. Another word for an entry that came into fashion in the fifteenth century is *vestibulo*.[17]

Neither Andrea Palladio nor Sebastiano Serlio used the word *corridor* in any significant way (Fig. 3).[18] In fact, they rarely even had anything akin to hallways in their designs, given that villas were always composed of tightly interlocked rooms. Even the radically enlarged Pitti Palace (1550s) built for the Grand Duke Cosimo Medici had no internal corridor. If corridors existed they were secret and for the most part not drawn into published plans. Such was the case of the *coritore* at the Palazzo Barbarini (1627–33) that, as documents indicate, went through the kitchen to the *piano nobile*.[19]

The emergence of the corridor into architectural daylight begins in the seventeenth century. A 1644 sketch for a palace by Felice Della Greca, a prominent architect practising in Rome, shows a *coritore* leading straight from the building's *entrata* to the *giardino* in the rear.[20] Taking the place of what would have been an *andito*, it had no overtly recognizable military purpose. Instead, it was clearly used as a status symbol, emphasising the importance of an owner who wanted to make the impression of needing to be kept abreast of world events by fleet-footed messengers.

The epitome of this was the false corridor that Francesco Borromini built in 1635 in the Palazzo Spada in Rome (Plate XV, page 84). Bernadino Spada, who was made a cardinal in 1626 and served as an important papal negotiator, had bought the palace in 1632 and hired Borromini to bring the building up to date, which he did by adding the corridor. Since only 8.5 metres of space was available for it, Borromini designed it with an optical illusion to make it appear significantly longer. Often discussed in the scholarly literature as a 'witty entertainment,' the most basic fact is overlooked, namely that it is a *corridor* that is being portrayed, with all this implies.[21] Placed on cross axis to Cardinal Spanda's reception room, lined with Doric columns and vaulted in a Roman, coffered style, it has all the appearance of a grand—and one has to add, modern— entrance-way into the palace, even though in reality it does not link to the street behind it. Clearly Bernardino Spada wanted to have the proper attributes of power, and in this case the illusion served just as nicely as the real thing. Bernini's corridor that led from his famous colonnade in front of the Basilica of St Peter in Rome to the Scala Regia (1663–6) would become the ultimate example of corridic display.[22]

These early corridors were show pieces and not an integrated aspect of palace design. Even Schönbrunn Palace in Vienna, built as late as 1696, had no corridors except as ancillary passages. So the question arises, when did the corridor become integrated into the architectural programme? When was it no longer something grafted onto an older building, but part of the working palette of the architect? It was Borromini, who made this transition, by designing the first example of what one could call a corridic building, namely the Oratory of Saint Philip Neri (1637–50) (Fig. 4). The corridors there form a large rectangle with a chapel clamped in the centre and the rooms of the institution lined up along the perimeter. The length of one of the corridors was extended to link to the entrance and as a result cut across the entire site. It separates the Oratorio from—yet connects it to—the pre-existing church and its associated rooms next door.

Borromini brought corridic logic to perfection at Sant'Ivo alla Sapienza (1642–50) where the U-shaped corridor system with its three entrances and co-ordinated staircase determined everything about the building, form, circulation and programme (Fig. 5). One could compare it with the design for the Collegio Romano, the centre of Jesuit education in Rome that was begun just a few decades earlier, in the 1620s, under the direction of Giovanni Tristano.[23] The contrast is striking. Whereas the Collegio consists of a series of Renaissance-style courtyards linked arbitrarily to each other and placed in awkward relationships to the church, Sant'Ivo's courtyard and church are subservient to the corridor system around which everything is organised.

The corridic revolution had now begun, but it was by no means widespread. Its first consistent articulations are in the context of the massive building campaign of the Jesuits, who built churches and colleges throughout Europe and in the New World. From the middle

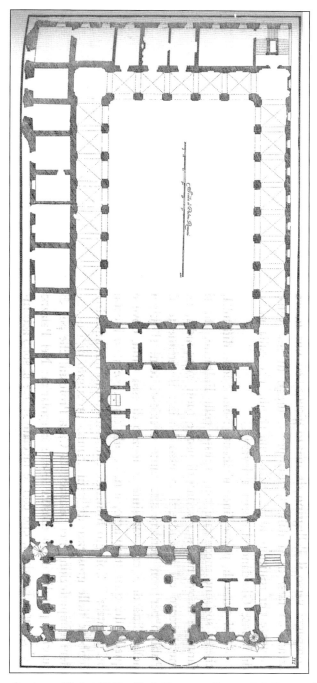

Fig. 4: Oratory of Saint Philip Neri, Francesco Borromini, Rome, 1637–50

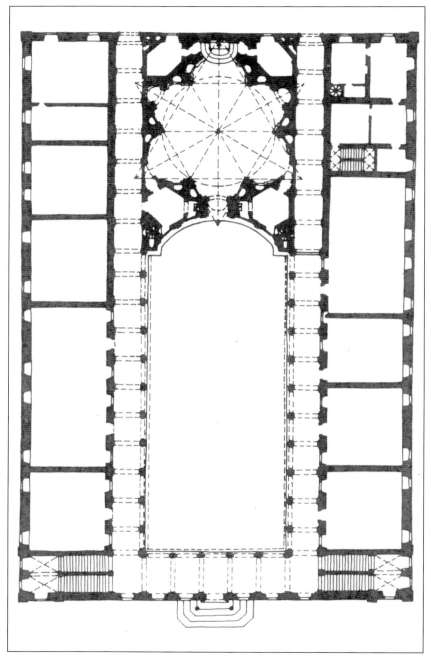

Fig. 5: Sant'Ivo alla Sapienza, Francesco Borromini, Rome, 1642–50

of the seventeenth century onward, in other words after Borromini, we consistently find *corridor*s running from a guarded street entrance into the depth of the college and its apartments.[24] Significantly, they are labeled thus in the official plans.[25] Not to be confused with a conventional cloister passageway, these spaces encode the building with the terminology of couriered messages, international power brokerage, and, by implication, Counter-Reformation alliances with Rome. They link the institution to the outside world in both real and symbolic terms. Few of these corridors posses the clarity of a Borromini building, but this only goes to show how difficult the transition was from the familiar courtyard system to the modern, corridic one.

Nonetheless, the shift in emphasis is real. In the old medieval and Renaissance system, one entered basically through the *andito* into a courtyard and from there into the building. In the new system, one enters directly into the building. The courtyard is still there for light, air and tranquility, as at the Jesuit college at Dubrovnik (Fig. 6), but it is no longer a circulation space. This corridic revolution spread to much of the new monastic construction especially in Austria and Germany, such as the Abbey of Saint Florian (1686–1751) in Linz (Fig. 7).

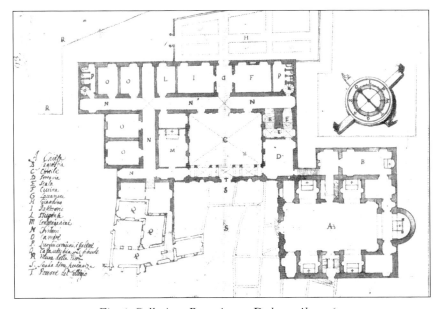

Fig. 6: Collegium Ragusinum, Dubrovnik, c. 1690

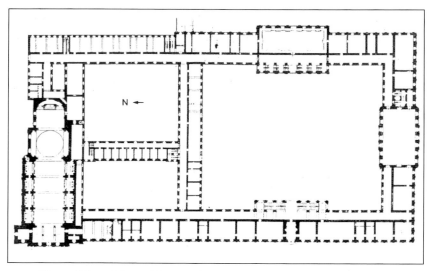

Fig. 7: Abbey of Saint Florian, Carlo Antonio Carlone, Linz, 1686–1751

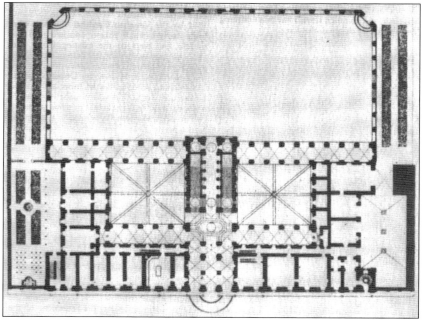

Fig. 8: Palazzo Corsini, Ferdinando Fuga, Rome, 1736

In an almost magical moment of transliteration, from walking to running, and from local politics to world politics, a new architectural element was born. The *corridor* emphasised not the dignified pace along an *andito*, but a pace that was much more purposeful. In seventeenth-century Italy, the corridor, therefore, had two identities, a virtual one that could be appended to a palace, as at the Spada, and a real one in the Counter-Reformation colleges and monasteries. Image and form were not yet co-joined. The first palace where they were unambiguously linked, though as separate entities, was at the Palazzo Corsini (1736) by Ferdinando Fuga (Fig. 8).[26] The entrance lobby led to a cross-axial corridor that linked the apartments on the far right and left of the building. Passing across that space, one enters into a narrower, axially-placed corridor that leads to the garden. It is articulated with semi-attached columns and is clamped between the arms of the grand staircase. It is one of the more brilliant plan-compositions of the eighteenth century, and might have had more influence had it not belonged to the last generation of great Italian palaces. But power had now shifted to England and with it the history of the corridor.

The English corridoor

About the middle of this staircase there was a corridor leading directly to the King's room. Gudden placed some of his keepers on the steps above leading to the tower, and himself stayed with the rest below, so that no one could be seen from the corridor . . . 'Suddenly,' writes Muller, 'we heard footsteps and a man of imposing height appeared from the door of the corridor and spoke in short broken sentences with a servant who stood near, bowing low.'
(William W. Ireland, 1889)[27]

The shift from an *andito* to a *coritore*, and then from a military term to an architectural one, might have been too subtle or perhaps even too regional to have had any lasting effect had the word not been carried to England.[28] Even so, it was not adopted in any wholesale manner. Instead it was used only in elevated commissions such as the huge Castle Howard (1698) built for Charles Howard, third Earl of Carlisle.[29] Designed by Sir John Vanbrugh, it has a great square hall with the principal apartments directly behind it. One stretch of space, labeled *corridoor* in the plan, cut across the front of the hall and curved around toward the side wings (Fig. 9). A second *corridoor* ran behind the hall to connect to the residential wing. Long thin buildings seem now to require corridors, but this was not felt at the time, as is easily proved if one looks at any number of other houses and palaces of that age. Petworth House, for example, despite its vast frontage, had no corridors, apart from the usual cramped passageways in the servant's quarters.[30] People moved, as was typical of the age, from room to room or along *enfilade* doorways.

Fig. 9: Castle Howard, John Vanbrugh, York, 1698

So why do *corridoors* appear in this building? It could be explained circumstantially by the fact that the English in Vanbrugh's generation, had a fascination for things Spanish. The English translation of Don Quixote, and the culinary dish 'Spanish olio', a mixture of meat and vegetables, had become all the rage in London.[31] Vanbrugh even wrote a play set in Spain, *The False Friend* (1709); perhaps more significantly, he was well trained in the military arts and rose, according to our sketchy knowledge of his life, to the rank of captain.[32] But the *corridoors* of Castle Howard have to be understood within a more specific perspective.[33] Howard was a prominent figure in the politics of the age. He was a minister for William III (1688–1702), a member of the Privy Council and also, briefly, Lord of the Treasury. To counter-balance the might of France, William III carefully maintained close relations with Spain, signing the Treaty of Madrid in 1670 and a Treaty of Windsor in 1680 and another in 1685, all aiming to rid the Caribbean of French buccaneers. The treaties also formally launched the English Caribbean expansion, with Britain taking formal control of Jamaica and the Cayman Islands thereby establishing a strong foothold in the lucrative sugar industry. The warm relations between England and Spain paid off in the War of the Grand Alliance against France with a victory for England and Spain. The war came to an end in 1697, one year before the commissioning of Castle Howard, which means that the building served purposefully, and ostentatiously, as a proclamation of England's arrival on the world stage. One of the attributes of an empire was a courier system, or at least its nomenclature.[34]

The same is true for the even grander Blenheim Palace (1705–24), which was also designed by Vanbrugh, this time with the help of William Hawksmoor (Fig. 10).[35] It was an unusual building as its construction was commissioned by Parliament to celebrate England's victory over the French in the gigantic, winner-take-all battle at Blenheim, Germany in 1704. The building was to be a monument both to the victory and to England's imperial future. Fittingly, it had *corridoors* leading from its huge main hall to the residential chambers. The drawings in Colen Campbell's 1715 *Vitruvius Britannicus* prove that these *corridoors* were unusual in so far as Blenheim Palace and Castle Howard were the only two buildings among the dozens featured in the book that had them.[36]

[113]

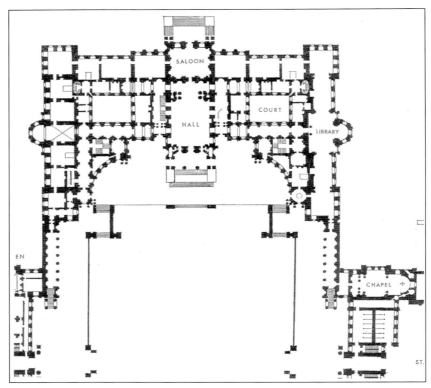

Fig. 10: Blenheim Palace, William Hawksmoor and John Vanbrugh, Woodstock, 1705–24

With their combined military and political symbolism, the *corridors* demonstrated, in the language of architecture, England's acceptance of the technology associated with its new status as a colonial empire, namely speed and connectivity.

It was left to Robert Adam, in a house now known as Luton Hoo (1772) in Bedfordshire, to tame the *corridoor* and coordinate it with the ideals of Italian planning (Fig. 11). The house was designed for John Stuart, 3rd Earl of Bute (1713–92). On the accession of George III in 1760, Bute became the King's Privy Councillor and for a while even Prime Minister (1762–3). He was called upon in 1763 to negotiate a peace treaty between England and France that ended the Seven Years War and established England as the world's chief colonial empire. Bute was, in the old sense of the word, a *corridor*.

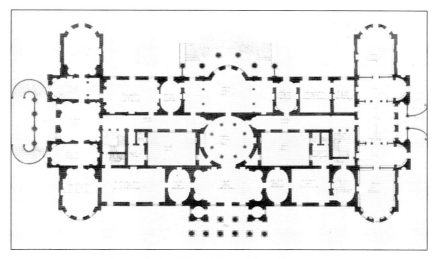

Fig. 11: Luton Hoo, Robert Adam, Luton, 1772

Luton Hoo, which served as Bute's retirement estate, was meant to commemorate his international career. A wide corridor—now spelled with one 'o' in the plans—cuts across the central axis and cleaves the house into two. It terminates at both ends in grand staircases.[37] The integration of the staircases with the placement of bathrooms, 'powdering rooms,' and service stairs was innovative, but as modern as it looks today, it would be a combination that would not be seen again at any level of frequency until the nineteenth century. To remind ourselves of the unusualness of the design we can compare it to John Carr and Robert Adam's Harewood House (1759–71) (Fig. 12). Though not dissimilar in layout, the passages around the two courtyards are not meant to be traversed by the house owners, but only by the servants.

The Earl of Bute was considered one of England's leading botanists, and his extensive library with some thirty thousand volumes—one of the most complete scientific libraries in Europe—dominates the entire right flank of the design. This was more than just a personal passion. Botany had not only risen to a science, but the study of plants, seeds and climate had become an essential element of the colonial enterprise.[38] The other side of the house contained a suite of reception and dining rooms, so that we have the social on the one side and the epistemological on the other, connected by the wide corridor.[39] The corridor, in other words, does not bring one into the depth of the building as at Castle Howard, but serves as a type of internal walkway. Unlike the earlier generation of corridors that led from the outside to the inside—whether in real or figural terms—this corridor connects two different insides to each other. Set apart from the rough and tumble world of politics, it was a protected space for restricted social interaction; It was a within in the within, a place where polite society could exercise its colonial dreams.[40]

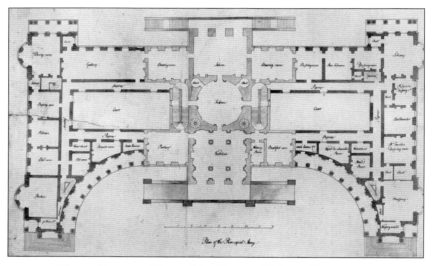

Fig. 12: *Harewood House, John Carr and Robert Adam, 1759–71*

The dark corridor

In eighteenth-century France one rarely saw the word *corridoor* anywhere on a plan other than in the servant's quarters, in theatres, hospitals, or, as we have seen, religious establishments.[41] As a 1769 dictionary states, 'Les corridors sont particulièrement en usage dans les Communautés réligieuses.' In domestic situations, they were a rarity. The primary circulation in a bourgeois *hôtel* went either along courtyards or through rooms. The bigger the *hôtel*, the more courtyards were needed. A project for a *grande maison* (*c.* 1780), designed by France's leading architect, Claude Nicholas Ledoux, maintained this convention (Fig. 13). The principal rooms were arranged in the form of an H around two large courtyards. It would have been anathema for Ledoux to have a corridor in the

[116]

CORRIDIC MODERNITIES

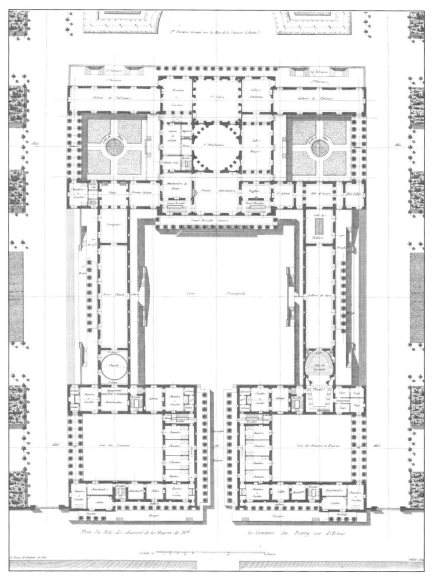

Fig. 13: Une grande maison, Claude Nicholas Ledoux, c. 1780

residence given that the spatial alignment of rooms was less important than the degree of intimacy which was created by the succession of ante-chambers.[42] For this reason, the definition of the corridor in Jean le Rond D' Alembert's famous *Encyclopédie* (1782) was far from neutral. It was not only inappropriate for a residence, but also a 'source of noise for the rooms opening off of it and, therefore, no longer in use except in upper stories of buildings meant for storage or in convents.'[43] As a result, the French made no significant contribution to corridic modernity. But they did contribute to the emergence of what we today would call privacy. It is often assumed that the corridor played a part in this, but the situation in France proves this wrong. What it shows instead is that the idea of the corridor and the idea of privacy were in the eighteenth century two separately developing modernities.

The corridor as a significant design element was to remain rare in France, even into the twentieth century. Beaux-Arts architects held firm to the Palladian courtyard tradition. They consistently used words like *galleries, colonnades, arcades,* or *colonnades couvert, dégagement,* but never *corridors.* The absence of the term is significant. Whereas a corridor could have rooms on both sides and emphasises speed and efficiency, a *gallerie* always had rooms on only one side and a row of windows on the other. A *gallerie* was a space for viewing the garden, or paintings, and for pleasant conversation and, importantly, leisurely ambulation.[44] Beginning in the eighteenth century, the French would begin to translate corridor as *couloir,* which was an old word meaning a water drain or sieve with clearly very different—and not positive—implications.[45]

England, meanwhile, was enjoying its own Palladian revival, so the corridic innovations at Castle Howard and Luton Hoo remained a rarity.[46] In fact, by the turn of the nineteenth century, the corridor came to be equated not with the world of international power-brokerage, but, if anything, with the nocturnal wanderings of old men in creaky mansions and with anxious perambulations in the dark. Rarely used in architectural discourses, the corridor seemed to be headed toward extinction.[47] Jane Austen never mentioned corridors in the great houses that form the backdrops of her novels, only galleries and passageways. Carlton House (c. 1795) had a corridor but it was out of sight in the residential suite (Fig. 14). As late as 1864, Robert Kerr, author of *The Gentleman's*

Plate XX: The Brumidi Corridors of the US Capitol Building, Constantino Brumidi, Washington DC, begun 1852

Plate XXI: Kilmainham Gaol, Dublin

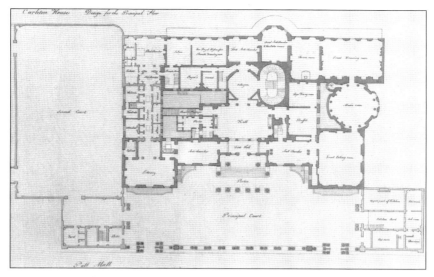

Fig. 14: Carlton House, Henry Holland, London, 1795

House, positioned the corridor lower in status to the French-derived *gallerie* because of its 'utilitarian character.'[48] The 'corridor' did survive, however, as a curiosity in gardens—otherwise known as a pergola, it consisted of a long trellised space covered with vines or other climbing plants that connected the house to the gardens or stables.[49]

The corridor's persistently negative—and still rather foreign—associations hindered its progress into respectability even at a time when civic architecture in England was beginning to develop. Well into the 1820s, courthouses did not have corridors or hallways. Lawyers and clients were expected to meet in nearby inns or coffeehouses.[50] Even grand buildings, such as Schloss Wilhelmshöhe in Kassel Germany (1792), the US Capitol (1793) (Fig. 15), the Massachusetts State House in Boston (completed 1798) and the Glyptothek in Munich (designed in 1815), the English Post Office in London (1823) had no corridors since their prototypes were for the most part French or Italian. The King Edward's School (1838), designed by Charles Barry, better known as the architect of the Royal Palace of Westminster, similarly had no corridors. With this in mind, the re-emergence of corridic space in the mid-nineteenth century is all the more remarkable.

SURGEONS' HALLS

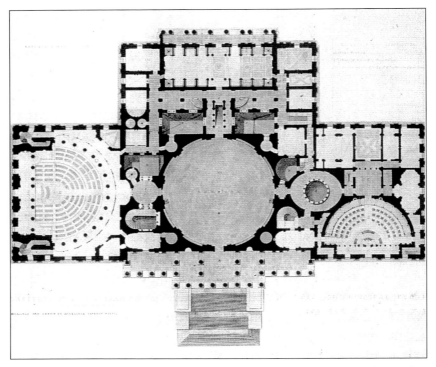

Fig. 15: US Capitol, plan drawn by Alexander Jackson Davis, 1832–4. Design by William Thornton, Stephen Hallet, Benjamin Latrobe, and Charles Bulfinch

The return of the corridor

> [The barracks] are compact and well built, and arranged on the corridor system, i.e. all the rooms open on to corridors, running the whole length of the building. (*Report of the Army Medical Department*, Great Britain, 1892).[51]

To follow the story of how the corridor acquired architectural legitimacy we will have to return to military history and go back to France where in the 1770s a new building type emerged, barracks, constructed at first not for the common soldier, but for the elite cavalry regiments. An early example dates from 1770 at a military camp near the town of Saumur, where a clearly labeled *corridor* defines the form of the entire H-shaped building (Fig. 16).[52] Apart from a rather modest entrance element representing the administrative centrality of the regiment's organisation, there is no 'space' in the building other than the corridor and its

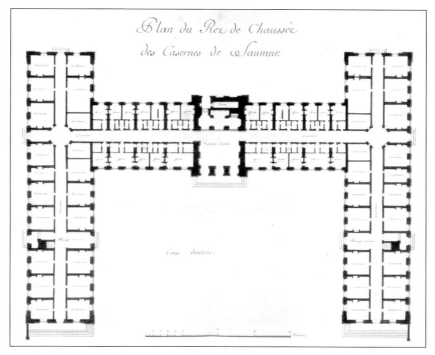

Fig. 16: Saumur Barracks, Saumur, France, 1763–5

associated rooms. Unlike earlier corridors which stood in the shadow of a church or of a suite of regal, state rooms, this one was the all-defining and autonomous element of the design. It is an anti-metaphysical space that cuts soldiers out of the natural order of life and family to reconstitute them into a new social order. This is, in other words, the first purely corridic building in the history of architecture and clearly the prototype for the modern corridor building.

Prior to the late eighteenth century, barracks were rarities. Soldiers bivouacked in the field or requisitioned the houses of citizens, much to the frustration of the Americans, for example, who listed this as a grievance in their Declaration of Independence.[53] During the American Revolutionary War, the English did eventually build barracks, but this was due more to the need to house large numbers of soldiers than because of any sort of ideological intent (Fig. 17).[54] The idea of the barracks as an ideological statement emerged only during the Napoleonic and post-Napoleonic era when it was tied in with the ideals of the nation state. The military vocation, which had been linked previously to the very definition of aristocracy and its blood lines, was no longer considered solely a privilege of birth, but now an attribute of citizenship. The definition of courage also went through a transformation. It was seen increasingly as a personal attribute, something that needed, however, to be organised in concordance with a larger purpose.[55] The French, of course, had been to the forefront of this, but it was not long before these ideas began to affect cultures elsewhere.[56]

The English, initially, were generally resistant to the value of barracks, since they appeared to encourage standing armies, which had been anathema since the wars of the seventeenth century. But the English were soon swept up in the transformations of the time and in 1792, Parliament consented to the setting up of barracks as an institution in the military command structure.[57] The Fethard Military Barracks for a horse-mounted regiment (Fethard, Co. Tipperary, 1805) and the grand Waterloo Barracks (London, 1830s), built by the Duke of Wellington, are only two of the more prominent examples. The barrack idea soon filtered its way down into the infantry. Not all barracks had inner corridors, but so many did that in Germany the term *Barackenstil* was used in the nineteenth century to refer to buildings—usually hospitals and schools—with inner corridors.[58]

Fig. 17: The British Barracks, Philadelphia, Pennsylvania, c. 1770

The corridic episteme

> On the other side of the corridor, we have Courts without end—half a score of them, that is, with as much difference between them as in the same quantity of oysters: some a little bigger than others, and differently marked on the shell; but very much alike in tout ensemble after all.
> (Charles Dickens Jnr, 'The Halls of Themis' 1883)[59]

By the 1820s, the elements of the modern corridor were beginning to come together as a spatial expression of the nation state and its ideals. The corridor was given an added component which it borrowed first from the Counter-Reformation churches in Rome and then from the art-filled *galleries* in France, such as those of the Louvre, both of which had made the corridor a destination in and for itself. One of the most spectacular examples was the corridor painted by Andrea Pozzo, beginning in the 1680s. Linking the Church of the Gesù to the rooms where St Ignatius had lived, the walls and ceiling of the unadorned corridor were decorated with trompe-l'oeil frescoes of classical architecture that framed pictorial dramatisations of the saint's life and times. The opening up of the fabled Louvre galleries to the public following the French Revolution added another layer of potential to these types of spaces.

The corridor's transition into the secular world took place, however, in England with two of the most celebrated commissions of the time, the redesigning of Windsor Castle and the construction of the new Houses of Parliament building.[60] As to the first, it was begun in 1824 (finished around 1840) under the architect Jeffry Wyatville, who unified the disparate elements of the building by means of a 170-metre-long Grand Corridor. It was so richly ornamented with furnishings and paintings that 'a day or two might be spent pleasantly' in this space, according to one nineteenth-century description.[61]

If this corridor, used for private occasions as well as public receptions, whetted the appetite for such spaces among the English, it was the new Palace of Westminster (housing the House of Commons and the House of Lords) in London that was the true watershed. Begun in 1834 and worked on for the next thirty years, it contains not one but several well-furnished, named corridors: the Commons' Corridor, the Chancellor's Corridor, the Lords' Corridor and so forth (Plate XVII, page 101).[62] Though these corridors were planimetrically linked, they were each a

SURGEONS' HALLS

discrete element with staircases at the ends that allowed monitors to control entry and exit. It was a brilliant solution to an important and emerging problem in mid-nineteenth-century English society, how to allow different classes to co-exist, spatially, in the same institution. In that sense, the corridor emerged from the increasingly complex social structure of Victorian society, introducing social stability and, very importantly, enforcing a sense of decorum in the inside of a public building. It guaranteed that everyone was in their proper position; awkward contacts with people outside of one's peerage were kept to a minimum. The corridor organised the world into different, but parallel corridic universes.[63]

The building that best represents the new episteme is the Royal Courts of Justice, designed by George Edmund Street (1873–82) (Fig. 18, Plate XIX, page 102). On the outside, the building has all the appearance of a hulking medieval castle and most descriptions emphasise this aspect of its design. The inside is a different matter altogether. There are not one but four different corridic systems. A private corridor for the bar circled the building between the courts and the central hall. Judges were provided with their own corridor, one-half level higher than that of the bar, that gave direct access to the raised daises on which the judges sat in the courts. The judges' corridor could be accessed from their carriages, and entered via a magnificent staircase, panelled in wainscot.[64] Another corridor accommodated barristers. The public had its own corridor, which connected to the upper galleries of the courtroom. Each corridic element had its own set of entrances, staircase and monitors. This building, in short, was a corridic machine.

Its design has to be seen in the context of the Reform Bill of 1832, that began the modernisation of English society, as well as the 1846 County Courts Act and the Judicature Acts of 1873, all of which tried to make the court system more streamlined and more easily understood, while at the same time expanding its reach. The old system of church courts was closed down and replaced by divorce and probate courts. The new court system also administered the increasingly voluminous legislation dealing with property, bankruptcy, succession, copyrights, patents, and taxation. The design of the building reflects not only these changes, but also the rise of the legal profession as a social sub-set with its own 'circulation system.'

[126]

CORRIDIC MODERNITIES

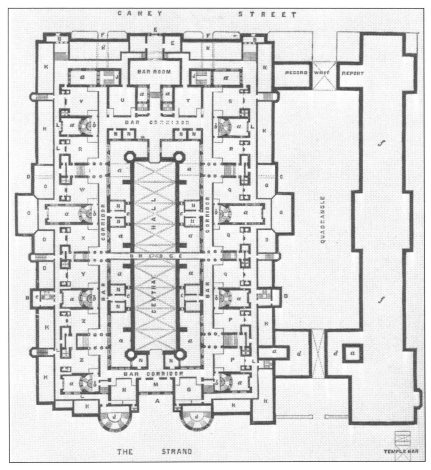

Fig. 18: The Royal Courts of Justice, George Edmund Street, London, 1870

As to the public, it too now began to take on a degree of importance and was no longer viewed merely as a bothersome horde. The word 'civilian,' brought over from France in the early nineteenth century, entered English parlance by the mid century. The civilian, one could say, was that part of society that was *outside* the corridor and its culture of expertise, but that was, nonetheless, impacted by the decisions that took place within the corridic institution. It is thus not incidental that the use of the word expert changed during this time as well. Prior to mid-nineteenth-century, a person was, generally speaking, 'an expert in' a particular field. By the mid century, we have the first recorded use of the word as a noun: 'the expert.'[65] The corridor was the space of expertise just as it was an instrument of surveillance, channeling and defining people into its spatial regimes.

Corridors soon became standard in town and city halls, in state houses and in governmental ministry buildings in both the US and Europe. Typical was the new United States Mint Building built in Philadelphia in the late 1890s under William Martin Aiken, the designer of dozens of government buildings. According to one description: 'The vestibule is highly ornate, the corridor extending through the cross section from east to west is finished in richly variegated marble. The floors are of messanine [sic; meaning here marble], the symbolic panels in the vestibule of glass mosaic. The ceilings are finished in white and gold.'[66] Even the US Capitol Building was outfitted—retrofitted—with a set of grand corridors with marble floors, custom-designed Corinthian columns, and vaulted ceilings painted with themes of law and governance (Plate XX, page 119).[67] The space linked the congressional library, the diplomatic reception rooms and various governmental offices. The Italian artist, Constantino Brumidi, who had established his reputation painting for the Vatican, was called in to make the frescoes on the walls and vaults. It took him twenty-five years. One of the purest corridic buildings of that era was the Rhode Island State Capitol (1895–1903), designed by the firm McKim, Mead and White, where there are two vaulted corridors flanking the central hall (Fig. 19). These corridors—and they are labeled corridors and not galleries—are intersected by two cross-corridors that as an ensemble define the shape and programme of the entire building. The central, domed hall is clamped into place by these corridors. In these corridors, which served as an in-between space in the modern political system with qualities that intermixed the private and public, a new breed of individuals was born, the 'lobbyists', who inhabited and animated this corridic world. A contemporary wrote:

> In the Latin, *lobby* signifies a covered portico-pit for walking, and in the Capitol at Washington the lobbies are long, lofty, and lighted corridors completely enclosing both halls and legislation. One of the four sides of this Lobby is guarded by doorkeepers who can generally be seduced by good treatment or a *douceur* to admit people to its privacy, and in this darkened corridor the lobbyists call out their members and make their solicitations.[68]

[128]

CORRIDIC MODERNITIES

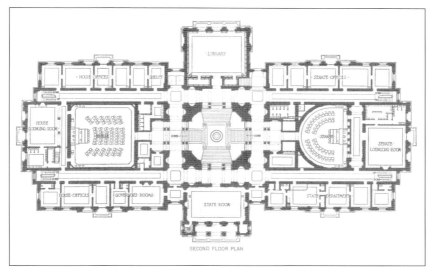

Fig. 19: Rhode Island State Capitol, McKim, Mead and White, Providence, 1895–1903

Needless to say, the lobbyists exploited corridic ambiguity for both good and bad. The philosopher, John Beattie Crozier, wrote disparagingly, in 1901, of 'the necessity of lubricants and persuasives to smooth the way [of politics]; and [thus] the appearance in due time on the scene of the Lobbyists, stalking up and down the corridors of Congress and the State Legislatures with bags of gold on which to draw at will.'[69] C. P. Snow's famous *Corridors of Power* (1964), which traces the attempts of an English MP to influence the country's nuclear weapons policy, could serve as a coda, expanding the corridor's metaphorical reach into the popular imagination.[70]

It was of course not only civic buildings that had sumptuous corridors: the new generation of corporate headquarters also borrowed the corridor element to add to the building's prestige. Such was the great corridor of the Cunard Building in Liverpool (1915) (Fig. 20).[71] The ground floor was divided by a sky-lit corridor six metres wide and sixty metres long, all in a Doric marble motif.

The corridors in these various buildings served several purposes. They defined the aspirations of a civic society under the supposedly enlightened leadership of its elites. They represented the epistemological revolution

[129]

that was taking place in office-work and governmental organisation. But they also represented the growth of the private sector and bourgeois culture in general. Corridors posed questions of etiquette, leading Emily Post in 1923 to write:

> A gentleman takes off his hat and holds it in his hand when a lady enters the elevator in which he is a passenger, but he puts it on again in the corridor. A public corridor is like a street, but an elevator is suggestive of a room and a gentleman does not keep his hat on in the presence of ladies in a house.[72]

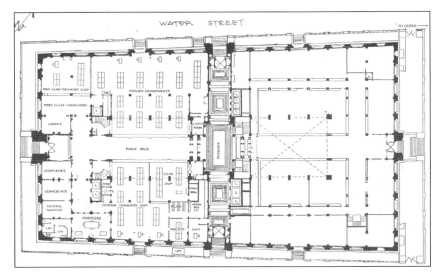

Fig. 20: *Cunard Building, William Edward Willink and Philip Coldwell Thicknesse, Liverpool, 1915*

Der Korridor

Despite the development in England and the United States of the corridor as a space of political and professional socialising and representation, it was not adopted for schools and universities, which were built resolutely around large rooms and halls, usually on a so-called pavilion model. A recent scholarly book on English schools built in the colonies prior to 1900, shows not a single plan with a corridor.[73] Equally, the French would never have put a corridor in a school. The schools designed around 1900 by Roger Bouvard (1875–1961) had long school rooms facing onto courtyards.

In Germany, where the word *Korridor* was assimilated into its language in the second half of the eighteenth century, the reception was unambiguously positive, so much so that at the end of the nineteenth century the corridic episteme underwent a major expansion of its significance. Why in Germany? Perhaps the fascination with England played a role. At the same time there was a distant relationship to the French Beaux-Arts and its antipathy to the corridor. At any rate, the *Korridor* became a key design element in Germany's new generation of universities. Karl Friedrich Schinkel's Bauakademie building in Berlin (1832–36) serves as a convenient starting point. Though it had a circulation hall around a courtyard, one would be hard pressed to call it a corridoric building. The circulation hall is in the style of an enclosed courtyard loggia and wraps itself so tightly around the courtyard as to leave it as little more than a vestige. But beginning in the 1860s, almost all of the major universities and research institutes—and there were many—had long, generously-scaled *Korridoren* that became an essential aspect of the institutional framework of German academe for decades.[74] The Berlin Poliklinik (1870) and the Physikalische Institute (1880) are particularly elegant examples. It is a U-shaped building with the operating room at its centre opposite the entrance. The corridors that emanate from the lobbies of these buildings tie all the spaces together. There is another aspect about these corridors that is important. Though clearly within the purview of the upper classes, these spaces were celebrated as social mixers.[75]

> When a visitor walks through the corridors of the two universities [in Zurich], he could, at least from the speech that he hears, not know in what country he is. (1895)[76]

This was a modernity of a brand new type, democratising, to some degree, the more restricted corridors of the English and Americans. No similar corridic revolution took place in English universities, and in France, the first academic corridor—*la galerie Richelieu*—was built at the Sorbonne only in the last years of the nineteenth century. The grand academic corridor was also quite alien to the university culture of the United States. Admittedly, McKim, Mead, and White designed a sumptuous, marble clad, Ambulatory Corridor of the Loeb Library of Columbia University (1896). But it was no *Korridor* in that it circled around the main hall. McKim, Mead, and White did use the corridor in

SURGEONS' HALLS

some of the university buildings that they designed, but because these buildings were basically conceived as 'pavilions'—which was the popular form of university building in the United States at the time—they cannot compare to the grand German *Korridoren*. The notable exception among the US universities was the design in 1913 of Massachusetts Institute of Technology which—modelled specifically on the German university—featured a wide corridor, that soon became nick-named 'the infinite corridor,' that ran through the entire building (Plate XVIII page 102).[77] For decades, until the construction of the Pentagon (begun in 1941) it was the largest corridic building in the world. The Lomonosov Moscow State University (1948–1953) designed by Lev Vladimirovich Rudnev brought the tradition of the sumptuous academic corridor to a close.

The modern, ventilated corridor

The problem with all corridors, regardless of how grand, was ventilation. 'There is,' according to a report on the Hounslow Barracks, 'a narrow corridor running from end to end down the centre, while from it on each side, open the men's rooms. To a person unused to them, and entering such rooms from the fresh air, the smell is unbearable.'[78] Throughout the nineteenth century, studies were made of ventilation with doctors decrying the increasingly common use of corridors in hospitals and prisons. 'The corridor,' according to one researcher, 'by communicating directly with two or more wards having deficient ventilation, allowed one ward to ventilated itself into another, and thus they became the means of a general contamination' of the whole building.[79] 'The evils connected with corridors may be seen . . . in almost every hospital in London.'[80]

The common solution was to use staircases as the lungs of the system. An injunction of 1899 by the leading designers of schools also wanted corridors to be 'of liberal dimension' and 'have an abundance of light and be cheerful in aspect;' adding that 'it is also desirable to give to them such decorative features and large proportions that they may express the noble purpose for which the school building stands.'[81] This was certainly the aim of the airy *Korridoren* with broad staircases that brought air up and light down that appeared in German universities. To avoid the build-up of foul air, the ceilings were usually made an extraordinary five and a half metres high.

By the end of the nineteenth century, the large-scale ventilation machines that were beginning to be developed were a natural fit with the corridor building. The engineer of the seventeen-storey Manhattan Life Insurance Building (1894) set the example by creating a system with basement fans that pumped air through large metal ducts that ran up along the elevator shaft and then branched off into the floors along the corridor.[82]

The totally enclosed corridor was finally possible and its advantages were immediately applied to a wide range of buildings.[83] Techniques were advanced so rapidly that Henry James in his book, *The American Scene* (1904–05) is greatly comforted by walking the 'long, cool corridors' of the Presbyterian Hospital in New York, even if they are 'halls of pain'. He admired 'the exquisite art with which in such a medium, it had so managed to invest itself with stillness.'[84] A leading physician in Germany could now argue unambiguously in favour of a corridor plan since it allowed for better ventilation, but also for more personal treatment, with two patients to a room, than the standard pavilion model with its jumble of interior spaces.[85] And indeed soon several major hospitals, such as the Frankfort City Hospital, were built as examples of the corridor system. The Royal Victoria Hospital in Belfast (1903) was one of the largest ventilated hospitals in the world to that date. Giant ducts worked their way from the basement along the corridor to the various wards, which hung off the central corridor like teeth on a comb. The mission of the system was not only to warm and humidify the air, but also to clean it of the soot in the outside air.[86]

George Widdows, a Fellow of the Royal Institute of British Architects and County Architect of Derbyshire (1905–36), in south central England, used the new ideas of ventilation and hygiene to create a novel form of schools that instead of having big halls, as was typical, had instead long 'marching corridors' which allowed for indoor exercise when outdoor space was unavailable or during periods of bad weather. One of the first schools of the new type was the Durnsford Elementary School at Wimbledon (Fig. 21).[87] The corridor, as its name implied, was not used for exercises in the contemporary sense, but for drill practices and synchronised motion.

'At the end of the course, the graduate should, with a little special training, be able to execute with ease most of the marching orders regularly performed by the infantry company . . . these gymnastics taught good discipline, quick response to command, better carriage; and also to make the pupil feel that he was one unit of a group and must act in harmony and unison with his classmates in order to secure success.'[88]

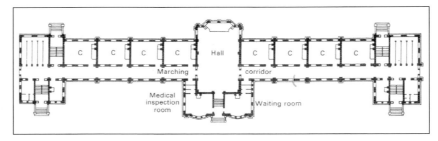

Fig. 21: Durnsford Elementary School, Wimbledon, England, 1910

Hundreds of such schools were built across England.[89] In due course the 'marching corridor' made it to the US. For William Butts Ittner, who designed dozens of schools across the United States, it had the added advantage that it served as a social space (Figs 22, 23, 24). In 1922 he wrote:

> It is a delight to linger in the corridor, since on the second floor it is a veritable art gallery . . . Altogether the school is a miniature democracy; high school students and primary pupils mingle in the most natural manner about the building and grounds. If training for the citizenship is a fundamental in education, the training, although to a certain extent incidental, is certainly in evidence.[90]

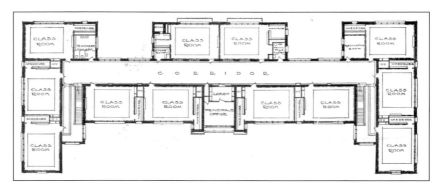

Fig. 22: William Clark High School, St Louis, Missouri, c. 1910

CORRIDIC MODERNITIES

By the mid 1930s the corridic revolution was in full swing, reaching its apotheosis in the 1960s in schools, apartment buildings (Fig. 25), and office buildings, where its former importance as a space of prestige and social differentiation gave way to generic linear spaces that facilitated the easy distribution of people and mechanical systems through the building. Its reception was still positive. According to one researcher,

Fig. 23: John Milledge High School, Augusta, Georgia, c. 1910

Fig. 24: Webster High School, St Louis, Missouri, c. 1910

[135]

the corridor 'helped reduce social stress because it gave a wider choice of spaces that were better defined as to ownership.'[91] Furthermore, unlike the more formal encounters in the state house corridors, in the context of the corporate office, a new type of corridic socialising developed, namely 'corridor conversations.' They were routinely praised. In 1971, a scholar noted that 'important occasions for listening, apparently, are corridor conversations, exchanges of ideas over lunch, chats at cocktail parties ...where senior men in the department get together with those whose work is being evaluated.'[92]

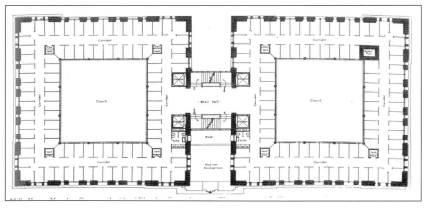

Fig. 25: Mills House, New York, Ernest Flagg, 1896

The anti-corridic movement

Modern materials, abstract detailing and the low ceilings of the post-World War II corridors put an end to the idea of corridic grandeur. Stripped of its vaults, frescoes, paintings, statues, and marble floors, the corridor, despite various claims still in its favour, slowly become a marker—one of many, of course—of what was wrong with modernism. Hospital designers, instead of seeing a space of hygiene and order, now complained that corridors 'interfere with normal verbal communication due to their characteristic acoustical properties.'[93] Educators, instead of praising the corridor's regimenting and democratising potential, now complained that corridors were a symptom of mechanised learning. Environmental studies, instead of proving a corridor's social effectiveness, now proved that they were isolating and stressful and that students who lived in corridor buildings 'tended to withdraw socially' and 'frequent mental health clinics.'[94] Sociologists, instead of seeing a tradition of personal interaction, saw only dark strips of wasted space that brought out the worst in people. Long narrow corridors and secluded stairwells were to be shunned, so one psychologist advised, since they elevated the levels 'of crime, drug use, vandalism and rape'.[95]

The first generation of anti-corridic buildings came, however, not from England or the United States, but from Germany, where architects, in the anxious post-World War II era, were looking for a socially-open approach to office design in opposition to the American corporate model. The *Bürolandschaft* (office landscape), as it was called, aimed to create a non-hierarchical environment that, so it was hoped, would allow for an increase in communication and collaboration. The floor plan of the Osram Offices, in Munich, designed by Walter Henn in 1963 featured a vast open floor with a chaotic jumble of desks. A few years later, the Dutch architect, Herman Hertzberger, designed the innovative Centraal Beheer office building Apeldoorn, Netherlands (1972) also without any halls and corridors. The building consisted of a series of interlocking blocks around open courtyards that made it impossible to walk in a straight line for very long. Instead of enclosed hallways, one had to walk near to, or even around, desks; walls were minimised allowing one see people in a variety of activities. The office workers, so it was hoped, would always be in touch with the pulse of human activities.

The critique of the corridor quickly expanded into mainstream architectural practice. The 1972 book, titled significantly *New Schools,* shows a consistent aversion to corridors and halls. The 'open plan' school, 'composed of broad expanses of enclosed space unbroken by walls,' became all the rage. Instead of spending money on 'walls and doors,' so it was argued, the emphasis should be on furniture and carpeting (Fig. 26).[96] Old-fashioned schools that did not fit this profile had their corridors and schoolroom walls removed. The Austrian-born theorist and educator, Christopher Alexander, added grist to the mill. In his book *A Pattern Language* (1977), which is still required reading in many schools of architecture, he argued that the rationalism of the modern age has 'so far infected the word corridor that it is hard to imagine that a corridor could ever be a place of beauty, a moment in your passage from room to room, which means as much as all the moments you spend in the rooms themselves.'[97] In 2002, professionals were still warning architects that 'spaces should be designed as streets, squares, and buildings as opposed to corridors, foyers and rooms.'[98]

The corridor received its most devastating critique from the English historian Robin Evans who, in 1978, argued that the corridor was instrumental in changing England in the nineteenth century from a society that had esteemed social interaction to a society built around the principles of privacy and personal segregation.[99] He pointed, by way of contrast, to the Italian Renaissance villa as a place where people had

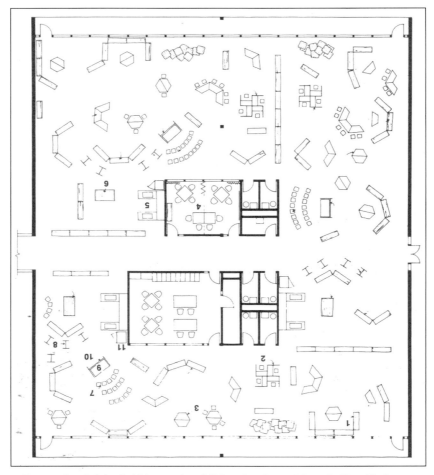

Fig. 26: Birch School Addition, Caudill Rowlett Scott, Merrick, New York, 1970

once intermixed in the interior spaces. As to the origin of the corridor, Evans attributes it, mistakenly, to the ascent of Puritanism.

Many architects now try to avoid corridic space. In the new Scottish Parliament building hardly any two office doors line up. Nonetheless, though the ideological supremacy of the corridor is no longer intact, it is certainly far from dead.

Corridic imagineries

The corridor's broad historical arc ran from its initial obscurity into the mainstream, and from its seventeenth-century position in the world of global empire to its twentieth-century position in the world of the global work place. From its inception the corridor was an instrument of modernity, relating first to speed, then to power, then to the regimentation of masculinity, then to emerging Victorian social structures, and finally, in the twentieth century, to hygiene, industrialisation and the corporatisation of life.

The corridor is also the site where the two concepts of interiority and modernity begin to overlap. Hegel defined interiority (*Innerlichkeit*) as the essential aspect of civilisational progress. Unfortunately for architectural historians, he never specified what that interiority in the modern age was to look like, *architecturally*, since he argued that the resolution was mainly in the discipline of poetry.[100] This did not stop those interested in architectural theory from attempting to extrapolate the Hegelian argument into the discipline.

Adding to the confusion was the tendency—latent within Hegel's Romanticism—to assume that interiority had to have psychological valences. Evans, for example, argued that because architectural space and psychological space are parallel they need to reinforce each other. Rational modernism and the corridor, so he felt, made that impossible. Sigfried Giedion, also heavily influenced by Hegel, was more optimistic about modernism, but this was because the Modernists used glass and large openings to obliterate the corridor and open up the building to the outside world, both physically and, so he hoped, sociologically.[101] More recently, Henri Lefebvre pointed to windows and thresholds as the key to architectural-philosophical meanings.[102] Following Gaston Bachelard, it is not the civic or corporate buildings that he sees as holding the promise for fruitful interaction between humans, but the conventional house, to be more specific, with windows, doors, attic and basement. In all of these examples, the corridor is either absent or a negative, and yet it is hard to discuss architecture's *modern* interiority—that is its alliance with the changing social and political realities from the seventeenth century onward—without it.

To put the the problem somewhat differently. There are two ways to address the disparity between the philosophical insistence on 'interiority' (as a trope of Romantic philosophy) and interiority as a topic in the context of architectural history. The first way, deriving from Hegel and reinforced by Evans and others, is that the corridor is a symptom of architecture's failure as a philosophical project and as such it brought about the inglorious end of a humanistic ideal as embodied in the Palladian (aristocratic) prototype. The alternative argument decouples the history of the interior from Hegelianist assumptions. The corridor created meanings through its attachments to aspects of our modernity that are distinctly anti-elitist, anti-metaphysical and above all public. The philosophical yearning for thresholds, windows and views, is, from the perspective of this alternative argument, an atavism. Philosophy wants to think anti-metaphysically, but live metaphysically.

Admittedly, the corridor did not always rise to the level of a particularly 'noble' revolution, allied as it was with the world of malodorous barracks, mindless bureaucracies, bourgeois politics and the white collar world of corporate management. But it stood, nonetheless, in dialectical relationship to the great halls of an earlier, aristocratic mindset. The corridor may not always match the great domes of old, nor demand the same type of architectural detail as other types of spaces, but once it had been freed from religious and princely metaphysics, it made possible a disparate array of structures: parliament buildings, state houses, school buildings, hotels, and office buildings that became the core—almost literally—of modern bourgeois, professional society.[103] And at the moment of its greatness—in the elegant and imposing corridors of the late nineteenth century—it was the intellectual and political space *par excellence*. The 'interiority' of the corridic institution was not a sanctum or retreat from the outside world. There is no ounce of domesticity in the corridor. For that one has to look elsewhere. The corridor was a

[140]

socially-defining place that in its post-Victorian incarnations beamed its efforts out into the world at large in the form of codes, management procedures, bureaucracies and scholarly publications.

Clearly the fracturing of the social fabric and the rise of individualism needs to be explained in the context of architectural history, but the corridor, despite the problems of 1960s, is hardly the culprit. In fact, until its demise, it created powerful cohesions. These cohesions were implicitly and explicitly opposite to those sought out by conservative forces in the nineteenth and twentieth centuries. Corridic cohesions were, in other words, not the family units that in the Victorian and post-Victorian age came to be so heartily championed, but purely modern ones, built around the nation state, class identities, bureaucracies, universities, corporations, hospitals and travel. Each developed its own profile in terms of belonging, enforcement, monitoring, and surveillance, but our critique has to start with the premise that the corridor was an armature around which a modern society could take shape, beginning already with the first, pace-quickening *coritore*.

Corridic futures

Today we talk of corridors of power, and of urban corridors, rail corridors, and pipeline corridors. In all this the meaning of the word, with its emphasis on speed, has managed to survive. What has also survived from its early associations with the Spanish Empire is the association of the word with modernity and the connection to the horizon. The word corridor manages to update itself with each escalation of reality, moving from body to building to pipelines. And it is also fitting that the word has left the field of architecture, where it exists only as a residual, to re-enter the realm of the geopolitical, where, in fact, it was born. In the late nineteenth century, a corridor in a state house *was* the locus of the geopolitical. Architecture today can no longer contain or adequately represent the corridic energies of our age, which have moved into the landscapes of the city, industry, and global capital. We speak now of 'development corridors' and 'migration corridors'. Even in the days of its inception, however, the purpose of the corridor was to put power in the hands of those who control it. In the global world, where new centres and new peripheries are continually being constructed, new types of

SURGEONS' HALLS

corridors are sure to develop. What had been locked into the interior of the building works now at a megascale and perhaps outside the bounds of representation.

Notes

1 It was badly restored after a fire in 1941. See Edward McParland, *Public Architecture in Ireland, 1680–1760* (New Haven, Yale University Press, 2001) p 110.

2 Robin Evans, 'Figures, Doors and Passageways', *Architectural Design* (1978) 48/4 pp 272, 278.

3 Anonymous, 'Review of Hester Piozzi's Travels through France, Italy and Germany.' *The Analytical Review; History of Literature, Domestic and Foreign,* Vol. 4. (London, J. Johnson, 1789) p 304.

4 William Chambers, *A Treatise on the Decorative Part of Civil Architecture* (London, Lockwood and Co. 1862) p 330.

5 Lord Byron, *Bride of Abydos, The Corsair, Lara,* (Paris, Baudry's Foreign Library, 1832) p 82.

6 Henry James, *The American* (Boston, Houghton Co. 1877) p 301.

7 Joseph Sharples and Richard Pollard, *Liverpool* (New Haven, Yale University Press, 2004) p 247.

8 *Tesoro de la Lengua Castellana o Española* (1611)—Edited and Reprinted by Martín de Riquer (Barceloa, S.A. Horta, 1943) p 363. Also Domenico Milco, *Il proprinomio historico geografico e poetico* (Venice, 1676) p 59. Also: 'Li Octo proposti et ellecti per la Coritore e Priore sianno confirmati all voce delli fratelli balontandoli.' [The Eight [council members] proposed and elected by the coritore and priors were confirmed by voice by the balontandoli brothers.] from a document dating from 1574. Published in *Gli Istituti Pii della citta e dell'antico Ducato Della Mirandola: Memorie e Documenti* Vol. 1, (Mirandola, Gaetano Cagarelli, 1882), p 91.

9 'La obsidione di Padua del MDIX', (1509) published in Giousè Carducci, *Scelta di Curiosità Letterari Inedite or Rare dall Secolo XIII al XVII,* Antonio Medin, Editor (Bologna: Romagnolie-dall'Acqua, 1892) p 98. In the fifteenth century, corridor could also refer to a speedy horse. See: Angelo Ambrogini [Poliziano], *Stanze* (1475–8), [1, viii, 6, and 1, xxvi, 3].

10 This from the Longfellow Edition [http://www.divinecomedy.org/divine_comedy.html]. I replaced 'vaunt-couriers' with corridors.

11 Adam Freitach [Freitag], *L'architecture militaire ou la fortification nouvelle: augmentée et enrichie de forteresses régulières, irrégulières, et de dehors, le tout à la practique moderne.* (Leide, Elzeviede, 1635) p 37; Antoine de Ville, *Les fortifications du Chevalier* (Paris, des Libraires du Palais, 1666) p 144. There are various spellings including *corredor, corridojo, corridoio, corritoio, corridore, coritore,* and *corritore.*

12 Giovanni Villani, *Cronica Universale,* p 227. Villani (1275–1348) was a historian

[142]

of Florence and a Florentine government functionary who authored this twelve volume history of the city: 'ma aggiunsevi per ammenda gli arconcelli al corridoio di sopra.' I would like to thank David Friedman for this citation. It is possible that the *corridoio* originated with the crusaders, who, often fighting against great odds, needed to move soldiers rapidly about the fortifications.

13 Rodolfo Lanciani, *Storia degli Scavi di Roma*, Vol 1. (Rome, Ermanno Loescher, 1902) p 91.

14 The French king Francis I had an underground corridor built between his palace and the residence of the aged Leonardo da Vinci. William Garrard in his book *The Art of Warre* (1591) writes: 'There shall be a Allie of 6 foote large, to receive the Souldiours which shall passe the great Ditch, to mount upon the Corridor of [the] Counterscarpe.' Cited in Charles Augustus Maude Fennell, *The Stanford Dictionary of Anglicised Words and Phrases* (Cambridge, The University Press, 1892) p 285.

15 A corridor—mentioned as such in the contemporary literature—was built in Parma to connect Palazzo della Pilota with a late medieval castle that was incorporated by the new Farnese rulers into a single palace complex. Though clearly not public, it was more than just an escape route, as it was 'nobilissimo e capacissimo.' Designed by Francesco Paciotto, it was built for Ottavio Farnese, Duke of Parma, who gained control of the city in 1551. It was completed around 1598. A visitor wrote that the 'corridore . . . è una parte del palazzo, che si è disegnato di fare, che sara nobilissimo e capacissimo, di qui abbiamo veduto il modello.' See: Helge Gamrath, *Farnese: Pomp, Power and Politics in Renaissance Italy* (Rome, L'Erma di Bretschneider, 2007) p 138.

16 See for example, Canto XXXIV of Dante's *Inferno*
'Non era camminata di palagio
là 'v' eravam, ma natural burella
ch'avea mal suolo e di lume disagio.'
[It was not any palace passageway
There where we were, but a natural dungeon,
With floor uneven and unease of light.]

17 See: Christoph Luitpold, *Frommel Der römische Palastbau der Hochrenaissance.* (Tübingen, Ernst Wasmuth, 1973) vol 3. p 184, illustration a; p 189, illustration b.

18 Palladio used the word once, but only to describe external, upper level connecting balconies. Andrea Palladio, *I quatro libri dell Architectura* (1601) p 16 or *The Four Books of Architecture* (New York, Dover, 1965) p 40.

19 A document from 1678, states 'Coritore nuovo sotteranio che dala cocina segreta pass all'Appartamento nobile.' See Patricia Waddy, *Seventeenth-century Roman Palaces*, (Cambridge MA, The MIT Press, 1990) footnote 373, p 399. In the *Dictionnaire de l'Académie française*, 1st Edition (1694), a corridor is defined as a 'termes de fortification,' and also as: 'Espèce de gallerie estroite qui sert de passage pour aller à plusieurs appartements.'

[143]

SURGEONS' HALLS

20 For an image of the plan see: David R. Coffin, *Gardens and Gardening in Papal Rome*, (Princeton NJ, Princeton University Press, 1981) p 161.

21 Jake Morrisse, *The Genius in the Design: Bernini, Borromini, and the Rivalry that Transformed Rome* (New York, William Morrow, 2005) p 256.

22 The use of the word corridor to describe these spaces is a modern convention. The documents relating to Bernini's designs talk of *bracciao* (arm). This according to Tod Marder who has worked extensively on Bernini's architecture.

23 Giovanni Tristano (active 1555–75) was a leading Jesuit architect of the time, who also worked for a period on the design of the Gesù, the Roman mother-church of the Jesuit Order.

24 See plan published in Richard Bösel, *Jesuitenarchitektur in Italien (1540–1773)* (Vienna, Verlag der Österreichischen Akademie der Wissenschaften, 1985), Illustrations 23, 29, 292.

25 Pietro Pirri, *L'interdetto di Venezia del 1606 e i Gesuiti; silloge de documenti con introduzione* (Rome, Institutum Historicum, 1959) p 159.

26 It was commissioned by Bishop Neri Corsini (1685–1770), on behalf of his uncle Lorenzo Corsini who had become Pope Clement XII in 1730.

27 William W. Ireland, *Through the Ivory Gate, Studies in Psychology and History*, 'The Insanity of King Louis II of Bavaria', (Edinburgh, Bell and Bradfute, 1889) p 152.

28 Ephraim Chambers, *Cyclopædia: or, An Universal Dictionary of Arts and Sciences:* Vol 1. (London, 1728) ' Corridor, in Fortification, a Road or Way along the edge of the Ditch, withoutside; incompassing the whole Fortification . . . The word comes from the Italian Corridore, or the Spanish Coridor.' (p 332)

29 Robin Evans discusses Coleshill House, Berkshire (circa 1650–67) as a corridor design. Even though the house has something akin to a corridor, the hallway is not labelled. The house was designed by Roger Pratt for his cousin, Henry Pratt, alderman of the City of London.

30 One could also compare Castle Howard with Burlington House (1665–8) by James Gibbs, which was, of course, modeled on Palladian villas where there were no corridors.

31 Edna Healey, *The Queen's House, A Social History of Buckingham Palace* (New York, Caroll & Graf, 1997) p 10.

32 A. E. H. Swen (ed), *Sir John Vanbrugh* (London, T. Fisher Unwin, 1896) p 22.

33 One also has to take into consideration that in the late seventeenth century military terminology had begun to spread in common language. Christopher Ridgway and Robert Williams, *Sir John Vanbrugh and Landscape Architecture in Baroque England, 1690–1730* (Gloucestershire, Sutton, 2000) p 55.

34 The word itself was so novel that during the design of Castle Howard, the Duchess of Marlborough, the wife of the building's patron, inquired about its meaning. Vanbrugh replied: 'The word Corridor, Madam, is foreign, and signifies in plain English, no more than a Passage, it is now however generally us'd

[144]

as an English Word.' The casualness of the explanation should not belie the implications of this innovation. See: Charles Saumarez Smith, *The Building of Castle Howard* (London, Faber and Faber, 1990) p 54.

35 It is thought that Hawksmoor designed the Berwick Barracks between 1717 and 1721.

36 A similar and also innovative corridor was added to the state room section of the Dublin Castle. It connected to the private rooms and was used as the ceremonial route for the privy councilors on their way to the main entrance to the council chamber (It was badly restored after a fire in 1941. See: Edward McParland, *Public Architecture in Ireland, 1680–1760* (New Haven, Yale University Press, 2001) p 110.

37 The building was transformed by Robert Smirke in the 1830s.

38 For discussion, see, Richard Harry Drayton, *Nature's Government: Science, Imperial Britain, and the 'Improvement' of the World* (New Haven, Yale University Press, 2000).

39 Another precedent, evoking the still very distant uses of the corridor in the twentieth century, was the Gloucester Infirmary (1761) where we see the emergent institutional culture adopt the manner of the grand house, radically simplified and modified, of course. Here the corridor links the two wards; the central hall has become the chapel with the operating room above it on the first floor. It was designed, so it has been argued, by Luke Singleton. The design was made around 1756. Patients were admitted in 1761. See: http://www.british-history.ac.uk/report.asp?compid=42309

40 The landscape and gardens were designed by the most famous landscape designer of the day, Capability Brown.

41 According to *Le grand vocabulaire François*, 'Les corridors sont particulièrement en usage dans les Communautés réligieuses.' See: Sébastien-Roch-Nicolas Chamfort, *Le grand vocabulaire François*, Vol. 7, (Paris, C. Pankoucke, 1769), p 73

42 Another comparison can be made with the Palazzo Corsini (begun in 1736) in Rome, which has galleries connecting important spaces and serving to define the structure's over-all geometry. Though here too there is a corridor, it is little more than a service-ally, squeezed into the fabric of the building.

43 Jean le Rond D'Alembert, *Encyclopédie* Vol. 9 (Paris, 1782), p 547.

44 In German, the prevalent word was *Gang*, which like *andito* is related to walking.

45 Jean-Hermann Widerhold, *Nouveau dictionnaire françois-italien et italien-françois* (Paris, Typographia Duilleriana [Duillier], 1677) p 197.

46 Walpole in Strawberry Hill constructed what today would be called a corridor, but he called it a Passage.

47 Though today scholars claim that panoptic prisons have corridors, Jeremy Bentham called them galleries. They were, however, no doubt corridor-like, but one has to remember that they were not circulation spaces, but optical spaces,

in essence free of circulation.

48 Robert Kerr, *The Gentleman's House* (New York, Johnson Reprint Corp., 1972) p 169. An example would be the Henry Latrobe designed Wyndham House, Salisbury from the early 1790s. It had a servants' corridor on the second floor that was, however, remarkable in having skylights.

49 It was used by Humphrey Repton (1752–1818) See: John Claudius Loudon, *The Landscape Gardening and Landscape Architecture of the Late Humphrey Repton* (London, Longman & Co., 1840) p 551.

50 Corridors could be found on the lower floor to connect offices, but this was driven by a need for the rationalisation of space rather than by civic purpose.

51 W. A. Mackinnon, 'Appendix to Report for 1890,' *Report of the Army Medical Department*, Great Britain (London, Harrison and Sons, 1892) p 347.

52 For a history of the building see: Éric Cron, 'La caserne des Carabiniers: une ambitieuse réalisation de l'Ancien Régime', *l'École de cavalerie, Histoire architecturale d'une cité du cheval militaire* (Paris, Centre des monuments nationaux, 2005) pp 49–73.

53 Sir William Blackstone, a noted lawyer and Parliamentarian maintained in 1765 that the soldiers should live 'intermixed with the people' and that 'no separate camp, no barracks, no inland fortress, should be allowed.' Quoted in William Edward. Hartpole. Lecky, *A History of England in the Eighteenth Century*. Vol 2, (London, Longmans, Green and Co., 1904) p 147.

54 Edwin G. Burrows, Mike Wallace, *Gotham: a History of New York City to 1898* (New York, Oxford University Press, 1999.) p 168.

55 Matthew McCormack, *The Independent Man: Citizenship and Gender Politics in Georgian England* (Manchester, University of Northampton, 2005). McCormack discusses the changing meanings of 'independence' from the British Civil Wars to the First Reform Act of 1832. The key shift was in who was thought to be capable of 'independence': once a state accessible only to legislators and those of rank, it came to consist of inner qualities considered critical for 'the electoral citizenry, and even the national repository of 'manhood' itself' (p 56).

56 In the decades prior to the French Revolution, the world in France was divided between aristocrats, the clergy and everyone else, the latter group known collectively as the '3rd estate'. In the Napoleonic era, the term '3rd estate' disappeared and people came to be known as 'citizens' tied conceptually to the state and to its successes and failures. Each citizen was potentially a member of the corps, a piece of the body of the state.

57 Chambers's *Encyclopedia*, Revised Edition, Vol. 1. (London, W. R. Chambers, 1886) p 708.

58 See, for example, Moritz Pistor, *Anstalten und Einrichtungen des öffentlichen Gesundheitswesens in Preussen* (Berlin, Julius Springer, 1890) p 228.

59 Charles Dickens Jnr, 'The Halls of Themis,' *All the Year Round, A Weekly Journal*. [London, 26 Wellington St] No. 736, New Series (January 6, 1883) p 9.

[146]

CORRIDIC MODERNITIES

60 The pronunciation of the word was debated, namely whether the accent was on the first or last syllable. See: 'Corridor,' *A vocabulary of such words in the English language as are of dubious or unsettled accentuation* (London, F. and C. Rivington, 1791). The house for the 5th Duke of Argyll, designed in 1803, was a rare exception, but its owner was a field marshal and commander in the English army. For image see John Harris, *The Architect and the British Country House 1620–1920* (Washington D.C., The A.I.A. Press, 1985) p 176.

61 'The Queen's Private Apartments at Windsor,' *Appletons' Journal: A magazine of General Literature*, New Series 7 (July–December 1879) (New York, D. Appleton, 1879) p 83.

62 It was designed by Charles Barry and August Welby Pugin. The inspiration for the corridors most certainly came from Barry.

63 Prestige corridors were soon to be found in the grand houses of the Victorian elites, mimicking the new corridic institution. Barry began to use corridors in some of his house designs, such as in Walton, for the Earl of Tankerville (1837) and Bridgewater House for the Earl of Ellesmere (1846). The latter, Francis Egerton (1800–57) was a patron of the arts and a politician with alliance to the Conservative Party. 1847 was the year he was elevated to the peerage as Earl of Ellesmere.

64 Anonymous, 'The New Law Courts' *The Law Times*, (January 13, 1883) p 189.

65 This astonishing fact is from the *Oxford English Dictionary*, p 432.

66 Frederick Converse Beach: Editor, *The Encyclopedia Americana* Vol. 5. (New York, The Americana Co., 1904) in the article 'Coinage'.

67 In 1852, construction began on the ornately decorated Brumidi Corridors on the first floor of the Senate wing in the United States Capitol. They were part of a new wing constructed by Thomas U. Walter. They are named after Constantino Brumidi, who created the paintings on its interior. Another example is the Town Hall of Leeds, England (1858). On the outside, the building has many of the conventions of historicism. We see grand columnar screens with Roman Corinthian columns. Its tower is reference to the Hellenistic monument of Halicarnassus. But inside there was a new phenomenon, the corridor that allowed—or at least hoped to indicate—the swift communication between the lawyers and the courtrooms.

68 George Alfred Townsend, *Washington, Outside and Inside, a Picture and a Narrative of the Origin, Growth, Excellences, Abuses, Beauties and Personages of Our Governing City,* (Hartford CN, James Betts, 1874) p 75.

69 John Beattie Crozier, *History of Intellectual Development on the Lines of Modern Evolution,* Vol. 3 (London, Longmans, Green and Co. 1901) p 303.

70 It became a widely popular metaphor, as, for example, Alexandra Smith, 'More women walk corridors of academia,' *The Guardian* (Wednesday 12 July, 2006) [http://www.guardian.co.uk/education/2006/jul/12/highereducation. uk1]; 'Clinton will stay out of corridors of power during trip to Africa' *The*

[147]

Mercury (August 04, 2009 Edition 2) [http://www.themercury.co.za/index.php?fArticleId=5111331].

71 It was designed by the firm Willink and Thicknesse.

72 Emily Post, *Etiquette in Society, in Business, in Politics and at Home* (New York, Funk and Wagnalls, 1923) p 22.

73 Lawrence Burchell, *Victorian Schools: A study in Colonial Government Architecture, 1837–1900* (Melbourne, Melbourne University Press, 1980)

74 Johannes Conrad, Ludwig Elster, Wilhelm Hector Richard Albrecht Lexis, Edgar Loening, *Handwörterbuch der Staatswissenschaften*, Volume 4 (Jena, Gustav Fischer, 1900) p 589–90.

75 See, for example, the Chemical Institute, built around 1866 in Berlin by Gustav Konrad Heinrich von Gossler and Albert Guttstadt. Plan in: *Die Naturwissenschsaftlichen und medizischen Staatsanstalten Berlins* (Berlin, Gesellschaft Deutscher Naturforscher und Ärzte. 1886) p 161.

76 'Wenn ein Fremder durch die Korride der beiden Hochschulen [in Zurich] geht, so könnte er an den Sprachen, die er dort hört, wohl schwerlish erkennen, in welschem Lande er sich befindet.' Zurich: unsere Hochschulen,' in Paul von Salvisberg, *Academische Review: Zeitschrift fuer das Internationale Hochschuwesen*, Vol. 1 (Munich, Academischer Verlag, 1895) p 500.

77 Though the building was designed by the Beaux Art-trained architect, William Welles Bosworth, the corridor was the product of the engineer, John Freeman, one of the country's leading civil engineers, who travelled to Germany to study their academic buildings before proposing his design for MIT. See: Mark Jarzombek, *Designing MIT: The Architecture of William Welles Bosworth* (Boston, Northeastern University Press, October 2004) p 33.

78 Author unknown, 'Our Soldier's Homes,' Examples of the Architecture of the Victorian Age, *A Monthly Review of the World's Architectural Progress*. (London, Darton and Hodge, 1862) Vol. 1. p 109.

79 'Sixth Report of the Medical Officers of the Privy Council, with Appendix, 1863' (London, 1864) as reviewed in 'Hospital and Hospital Construction' *The American Journal of Medical Sciences* (Philadelphia, Henry C. Lea, 1868) New Series Vol. 56, p 198. See also: Walker Gill Wylie, Hospitals: their History, Organization, and Construction (New York, D. Appleton, 1877) p 205.

80 Anonymous, 'The Sanitary Condition and Construction of Hospitals,' *The Lancet* (London) 2/4, 1859, p 345.

81 Severance Burrage, Henry Turner Bailey, *School Sanitation and Decoration* (Boston, D. C. Heath, 1899) p 21.

82 'Power and Heating Plant, Manhattan Life Insurance Building,' *American Steam and Hot-water Heating Practice*, (New York, The Engineering Record, 1894) p 212–17. The architects were Kimball and Thompson and the engineer, Charles Sooysmith. It was demolished in 1930.

83 For attempts to solve this, see: *Transactions of the American Society of Heating*

and Ventilating Engineers Vol. 18 (New York, American Society of Heating and Ventilating Engineers, 1912) pp 398–400. The society was formed in 1895. Ducting in buildings came on gradually. Even the fifty-seven story high Woolworth Building (1910–13) in New York had ceiling heights between 12 and 20 feet and no ducting.

84 Henry James, *American Scene* (London, Chapman & Hall, ltd., 1907) p 140–1.

85 Ernst Beyer, 'Die Heilstättenbehandlung der Nervenkranken,' *Zentralblatt für Nervenheilkunde und Psychiatrie*, Vol. 19 (1908) p 715. For a discussion about the corridor see, Hermann Lenhartz, *Der moderne Krankenhausbau vom hygienischen und wirtschaftlich-technischen*, (Braunschweig, Friedrich Wieweg, 1908) p 46–7.

86 For a discussion see: Raynar Banham, *The Architecture of the Well-tempered Environment*, second edition, (Chicago, University of Chicago Press, 1984, pp 80–82.)

87 http://www.aboutderbyshire.co.uk/cms/people/george-widdows-schooldays. shtml

88 Norman Zafros, 'The Place of Tactics in Public School Gymnastics,' *American Physical Education Review* 221/7, Edited by James Huff McCurdy (October, 1916) p 411.

89 'A new Board[ing] school has been opened in Central Road, Blackpool . . . The building is of two floors with a marching corridor 12ft. wide in the centre of each floor, having the classrooms grouped round it and entering directly from it.' Anonymous, 'General Building News,' *The Builder* 82/3089 (April 19, 1902) p 401.

90 William B. Ittner, 'The School Plant in Present-Day Education,' *The Architectural Forum* 37/2 (August 1922) p 50. Ittner (1864–1936) was an architect practising in St Louis and Commissioner of School Buildings for the Board of Education. Ittner served in that position until his resignation in 1910. He continued as 'consulting architect' to the Board until October of 1914. In addition to the fifty school buildings in St Louis that Ittner's firm produced, there are hundreds of school buildings in over twenty-five other states.

91 Gary W. Evans, *Environmental Stress* (Cambridge, Cambridge University Press, 1982) p 159.

92 Richard Leslie Larson, *The Evaluation of Teaching College English* (New York, Modern Language Association of America, 1971) p 56.

93 M. Spivack, 'Sensory Distortion in Tunnels and Corridors,' *Hospital and Community Psychiatry*, 18, No. 1, January, 1967.

94 Dennis Coon, John O. Mitterer, *Introduction to Psychology* 12th edition, (Andover, GB, Thomas Learning, 2009) p 600.

95 Grahame Hill, *A-Level Psychology Through Diagrams* (Oxford, Oxford University Press, 2001) p 277. The book that stated this critique was; Oscar Newman, *Defensible Space: Crime Prevention through Urban Design* (New York, Collier Books, 1973).

96 Anonymous, *Places and Things for Experimental Schools* (New York, Education Facilities Laboratories, 1972) p 22, 44.

97 Christopher Alexander, *A Pattern Language* p 633.

98 Brian Edwards, *Libraries and Learning Resource Centres* (Oxford, Architectural Press, 2002) p 46.

99 Robin Evans, 'Figures, Doors and Passageways', *Architectural Design* (1978) 4: 267–78.

100 For more on this see: Mark Jarzombek, 'The Cunning of Architecture's Reason,' *Footprint 1*, (Autumn, 2007) pp 31–46.

101 Sigfried Giedion, who derives his argument very clearly from Hegel (*Space Time and Architecture*, Cambridge, Harvard University Press, 1941) sees the history of interiority as beginning with the Romans and then, after the Middle Ages, descending rapidly, ending in 'the tragic history of the nineteenth century' (p 562). Interiority was redeemed only with the likes of Mies van der Rohe and Walter Gropius.

102 Henri Lefebvre, *The Production of Space* (Oxford, Blackwell, 1991) p 210.

103 If there was one type of work that was suited to corridic modernity from the late nineteenth century onward, it was the office worker, and later the women in the secretarial pool—what we now call 'white collar.' The term was first used by Upton Sinclair in 1919, but research in it only developed in subsequent decades. See: Charles Wright Mills *White Collar: The American Middle Classes* (Oxford, Oxford University Press, 1951).

Photograph acknowledgements

Fig. 1: Frank Salmon, *Building on Ruins* (Aldershot, Ashgate, 2000) p 202.

Fig. 2: Ibid., p 217.

Fig. 3: Andrea Palladio, *The Four Books of Architecture* (New York, Dover, 1965) Plate 45.

Fig. 4: Francesco Borromoni, *Opera del Francesco Boromino* (Rome, Edizioni dell'Elefante, 1964) p 27.

Fig. 5: Anthony Blunt, *Borromini* (Cambridge, Harvard University Press, 1979) p 113.

Fig. 6: Richard Bösel, *Jesuitenarchitektur in Italien (1540–1773)* Vol. 2 (Vienna, Verlag der Österreichischen Akademie der Wissenschaften, 1985) p 29.

Fig. 7: Günter Bruche, *Barock Architectktur in Österreich* (Cologne, DuMont, 1983) p 69.

Fig. 8: Anthony Blunt, *Guide to Baroque Rome* (New York, Harper & Row, 1982) p 176.

Fig. 9: James Lees-Milne, *English Country Houses: Baroque, 1685–1715* (London, Country Life Books, 1970) p 159.

Fig. 10: Kerry Downes, *English Baroque Architecture* (London, A. Zwemmer, 1966) Fig. 37.

CORRIDIC MODERNITIES

Fig. 11: Damie Stillman, *English Neo-Classical Architecture* Vol. 1 (London, A. Zwemmer, 1988) p 145.

Fig. 12: Ibid., p 92.

Fig. 13: Claude Nicholas Ledoux, *Architecture de C. N. Ledoux* Vol. 1 (Paris, Lenoir, 1847) plate 169.

Fig. 14: Stillman op. cit. p 186.

Fig. 15: Dell Upton, *Architecture in the United States* (Oxford, Oxford University Press, 1998) p 72.

Fig. 16: Pierre Garrigou Grandchamp, Saumur. *l'École de cavalerie, Histoire architecturale d'une cité du cheval militaire* (Paris, Centre des monuments nationaux, 2005) p 70.

Fig. 17: John F. Watson, *Annals of Philadelphia and Pennsylvania in the Olden Time*, Vol. 1, (Philadelphia, Carey and Hart, 1845) page opposite 412.

Fig. 18: John Summerson, *Victorian Architecture* (New York, Columbia University Press, 1970) p 108.

Fig. 19: McKim, Mead & White, *Monograph of the work of McKim, Mead & White, 1879–1915* (New York, Arno Press, 1977) p 183.

Fig. 20: Richard A. Fellows, *Edwardian Architecture* (London, Lund Humphries, 1995) p 113.

Fig. 21: Malcome Seaborne and Roy Lowe, *The English School, its Architecture and Organization*, Vol. II 1870–1970 London, Routledge and Kegan, 1977, p 89.

Fig. 22: Fletcher B. Dresslar, *American Schoolhouses*, Washington DC, Government Printing Office, 1911, plate 173.

Fig. 23: Ibid., plate 23.

Fig. 24: Ibid., plate 24.

Fig. 25: Robert Stern, *New York 1900: Metropolitan Architecture and Urbanism, 1890–1915* (New York, Rizzoli, 1983) p 279.

Fig. 26: James J. Morisseau, *The New Schools* (New York, Van Nostrand Reinhold, 1972) p 11.

Plate XIV: Terence Meade's photostream http://www.flickr.com/photos/jacks-coldsweat/2563342498/

Plate XV: Roy Reed

Plate XVI: http://www.flickr.com/photos/19178753@N04/3538079877/

Plate XVII: Wikicommons (British Library)

Plate XVIII: Mark Jarzombek

Plate XIX: Barbara Rich

Plate XX: Jack Mayer

Plate XXI: Mark Jarzombek

Fig. 1: The obelisk and fountain at the main entrance of Royal College of Surgeons in Ireland-Medical University Bahrain

Royal College of Surgeons in Ireland-Medical University of Bahrain, 2009

Colin Stewart

'In a sense each of us is an island. In another sense, however, we are all one. For though islands appear separate, and some may even be situated at great distances from one another, they are only extrusions of the same planet Earth.'
J. David Walters

On Tuesday, 3 February 2009, 199 years after the opening of its first building on St Stephen's Green, the Royal College of Surgeons in Ireland passed another milestone in its history when the President of Ireland, Mary McAleese, on an official visit to Bahrain, opened the new Royal College of Surgeons in Ireland-Medical University of Bahrain campus in the presence of His Highness Shaikh Khalifa Bin Salman Al Khalifa, Prime Minister of the Kingdom of Bahrain (Plate X, page 65).

Bahrain and RCSI

Bahrain is a small archipelago of 33 islands located off the eastern coastline of Saudi Arabia in the Arabian Gulf, with a total land area of 700 square kilometres. Modern causeways connect the four main islands, and all are connected to Saudi Arabia by the 16-mile-long King Fahd Causeway. The largest island is Bahrain Island. Its name is derived from two Arabic words 'thnain bahr' meaning 'two seas'. This name refers to the phenomenon of sweet water springs under the sea, which mingle with the salty seawater. Many natural freshwater springs once irrigated the fertile northern and western areas of Bahrain from underground aquifers, but these resources are finite and estimates suggest they will not last another fifty years. Of the current population of 730,000, some 160,000 are concentrated around Manama, the capital city, and about 30 per cent are non-Bahraini immigrants.

[153]

Like other Gulf states, Bahrain had a long relationship with the United Kingdom, until declaring its independence in 1971 when it also joined the United Nations. The Royal College of Surgeons in Ireland's relationship with Bahrain goes back for nearly thirty years to just after the country's independence. It has involved the delivery of training programmes in surgery, family practice and healthcare management as well as postgraduate surgical examinations and supporting preparatory courses.

The current initiative began when Dr Faisal Al Mousawi, current President of RCSI-Bahrain and former Minister of Health and President of the Shura Council, attended the College's overseas meeting in Penang in 2000 and, having considered the development of Penang Medical College, posed the question: 'why don't you do this in Bahrain?' Over the next two or three years the idea germinated and grew, with the close support of the Bahraini government. In October 2003, a Memorandum of Understanding was signed with His Highness the Prime Minister of Bahrain, Shaikh Khalifa Bin Salman Al Khalifa, a keen supporter of the initiative, requiring the College to undertake a feasibility study on the establishment of a medical university in Bahrain (Table 1). The College Finance Committee considered the study at its meeting in January 2004 and expressed its strong support for the plan. At this time, the projections envisaged 1,350 students in all disciplines, that is, medicine, nursing, physiotherapy, pharmacy, dentistry and healthcare management. The establishment of a medical undergraduate programme was the priority and the target intake for the first year was 50 students. Through the patronage of Shaikh Khalifa Bin Salman Al Khalifa, the Royal College of Surgeons in Ireland-Medical University of Bahrain was formally founded in 2004 under licence from the Government of the Kingdom of Bahrain.

Mercury Engineering, through its subsidiary Mercury Middle East, was an established and growing enterprise in Bahrain and the Gulf region. In 2003 a chance conversation took place between Frank O'Kane, Chairman and Chief Executive of Mercury Holdings, and Michael Horgan, on the College's aim to establish a medical university on the island. Frank, a well known supporter of education in Ireland and aware of the limited time available to RCSI, offered his company's

[154]

assistance with getting the proposed university established. This offer was taken up and Mercury Engineering was engaged to take forward and manage a number of aspects of this project. Pearse Cole, Mercury's project director, was appointed to make it all happen.

The first job was to deliver, within an extremely tight time frame, the fit-out of RCSI-Bahrain's temporary campus in the Al Saffar Building in the Seef district. The second was to project-manage the design and tender stages of proposals for the permanent campus in Busaiteen. The final role undertaken was as the main contractor for the construction and delivery of the first phase of the new campus. This was a novel departure for Mercury Engineering as they were known for their strong reputation as mechanical and electrical subcontractors, but not as construction contractors. However the 'can do' attitude which was evident in the delivery of the Seef campus was brought to bear on the Busaiteen site. Under Pearse's direction, Mercury assembled a unique project team which in a very short time took an extremely personal pride in the project and demonstrated in many ways a determination to make the exercise a success.

For the initial intake a shell building was identified in the Seef District; two floors were leased, the layout agreed and the necessary work carried out over the summer of 2004 in time for the first intake in October. The new medical school was officially opened in October 2004 by His Highness the Prime Minister of the Kingdom of Bahrain, Shaikh Khalifa Bin Salman Al Khalifa and the Taoiseach of Ireland, Mr Bertie Ahern TD. Twenty-seven students, from Bahrain, India, Italy, Kuwait, Pakistan, Saudi Arabia, United Arab Emirates, United States of America and Yemen, were admitted to the inaugural foundation year for medicine in October 2004. By October 2009 there were students of 34 nationalities represented in the student body.

At the same time the concept and design brief for a permanent campus was being advanced. A number of critical issues had to be resolved as the design progressed, notably the location of the permanent campus and the availability of undergraduate and postgraduate clinical training places. In the event, these two questions had a common resolution.

As with any medical school, the availability of suitable clinical training places is paramount in the delivery of the programme and the production

[155]

of graduates of high quality. The two principal training hospitals on the island, Salmaniya Hospital and the Bahrain Defence Forces Hospital, had accommodated medical students and graduates from established programmes on the island and could cope with some modest expansion, but not with the numbers which were envisaged once RCSI-Bahrain was at full capacity. Luckily, a new general hospital was already planned for the Busaiteen area on Muharraq Island. The synergy of having the RCSI School of Medicine close by was obvious and through the good auspices of the Royal Court, the College was gifted the land next door to the site of the proposed new hospital, which was to be known as the King Hamad General Hospital.

The suggested site lay immediately to the north of the Sheikh Isa Bin Salman Causeway, close to Bahrain International Airport and near to the city centre of Manama south of the causeway. There was one problem—the land in question was on the sea bed of the Arabian Gulf. By January 2005, however, the land had been fully reclaimed and infilled. It was still settling, but at a level above mean sea level and higher than early predictions. This was typical of the swiftness with which the whole project was moving.

On 13 March 2006 the foundation stone for the new Royal College of Surgeons in Ireland-Medical University of Bahrain campus in Busaiteen, Muharraq, Bahrain was jointly laid by His Highness the Prime Minister of Bahrain, Shaikh Khalifa Bin Salman Al Khalifa and the Tánaiste and Minister for Health and Children in Ireland, Ms Mary Harney T.D.

The campus concept

The aim of the first phase of construction of the new permanent campus was to accommodate 600 students and staff with some room for expansion. The design, tender and construction programme envisaged occupation in the autumn of 2007.

From September 2004, the design team of Aedas (master planning) and Mohamad Salahuddin Consulting Engineering Bureau (MSCEB), architects and engineers, worked to meet the College's wish for a modern, prominent and distinctive campus that would exude quality to passers-by and become a centre of excellence in international medical teaching. Co-located with the King Hamad General Hospital, it offered the opportunity to be part of a cohesive strategy for medical provision on the two sites with the potential for future expansion. It was also important that the campus should reflect the coming together of the two cultures and identities, Bahraini and Irish, in this unique development.

There has been a human presence on Bahrain for at least 7,000 years. Pottery shards found amongst Stone Age flints suggest the growing strategic importance of the archipelago as a source of sweet water for sea-going travellers from the 5th millennium to the 3rd millennium BCE. The Barbar Temple demonstrated the high degree of civilisation the Bahraini population had reached by the 3rd millennium. It was excavated in the 1950s. The temple consists of three distinct layers built at different stages in a style similar to that found in Mesopotamia (Iraq). Considering an appropriate theme for the campus, the Irish contingent immediately thought of Newgrange, constructed in Ireland around the same time period.

Newgrange was built between *c.* 3,300 and 2,900 BCE by neolithic farmers, who possessed considerable expertise in engineering, architecture, art and astronomy. Like the Barbar Temple, Newgrange is some five hundred years older than Stonehenge and indeed older by several centuries than the Great Pyramid of Giza in Egypt. A World Heritage Site, the monument is a megalithic passage tomb consisting of a kidney shaped mound covering an area of over one acre and is surrounded by 97 kerbstones, some of which are richly decorated with megalithic art. The 19 metre long inner passage leads to a cruciform chamber with a corbelled roof. A unique feature of the construction is its deliberate orientation on the north bank of the Boyne valley towards the southeast. At sunrise on mid-winter's day, the passage and chamber of Newgrange are illuminated for a short time by the sun's rays passing through the light box above the entrance.

The design team came over to Ireland from Bahrain and spent some time visiting Newgrange. Thus stimulated, the design team was able to translate their early ideas into a structured, themed conceptual design which would capture many of the characteristics and images of both islands' art, history and culture.

[157]

SURGEONS' HALLS

The campus and the project

The campus comprises approximately 24 acres. The master plan of the structures on the site follows a zoning strategy comprising the central core teaching areas, additional school buildings which can be developed in phases and will radiate from this central core, residential and sports and recreational facilities with service buildings located at the perimeter. At the centre of the complex, a sculpture contains lighting elements representing the 'light of knowledge' which shines out from the obelisk sited on top of a water feature (Fig. 1).

The initial development has been confined to the central core teaching area or core building, the sports hall and service buildings. Cost restrictions have forced the downsizing of the core building, but it is still of sufficient space to accommodate common teaching areas, student support services, learning resources, shared office accommodation and recreational spaces over five levels (Table 2). Normal access is at ground level from the car parks via a service roadway under the building and through stair and lift wells at either end of the building. A stylised ramp from ground level leads to the main entrance at level 1. The main entrance gives access to the atrium which receives diffused natural light through a Teflon coated high tensile fibreglass fabric roof awning. The atrium provides access to lecture theatres, clinical skills suites, laboratories and administrative and academic offices (Plate XI, page 65). On level 2 there are multipurpose laboratories and administrative and academic offices. The majority of administrative and academic offices, a large seminar/tutorial room and the Stephen's Green restaurant can be found on level 3. Level 4 hosts five tutorial rooms (three of which can be divided), a large seminar/ tutorial room and the Frank O'Kane Learning Resource Centre. The university executive and office bearers are located on level 5 together with the Board Room and a smaller meeting room. To the southeast of the site lies the sports hall.

From the autumn of 2004, when the design work began, to the winter of 2005/2006 the project design team refined the plan for the site, the building, structural, mechanical and electrical design and developed the various tender packages. The piling contract for the core building, sports hall and the first accommodation block was awarded in February 2006 with piling commencing on 18 March, following the foundation stone

[158]

laying ceremony, and completed in May. Main contract tenders were issued on 19 February 2006 with an initial submission date of 9 April, but this was postponed until 14 May due to extraordinary time pressures in the local market as a consequence of other major tenders and associated value-engineering requirements. Aware of the booming construction market in Bahrain at this time, as well as worldwide inflationary pressures potentially affecting the costs of specialist labour and raw materials, the RCSI team wanted to ensure that it was protected against these upward costs during the life of the construction and that it was getting value for money. Although the tenders had been evaluated by July 2006 and a preferred contractor identified, protracted financial and contractual discussions took place until November as the College put in place the necessary measures to address their concerns. These were concluded by early December and the civil engineering and construction contractor, G. P. Zachariades, took possession of the site on the 15 December 2006.

By the middle of January 2007, mobilisation was well advanced and the works on pile trimming had commenced. Although the project was now underway, it was clear that the original deadline of the autumn of 2007 was no longer possible. The project had a programme life of 80 weeks, which gave a target handover date to the College of 11 August 2008. In practice the handover of the core building and the service buildings took place on 11 September with the new academic session beginning on Sunday 5 October 2008 (Table 4).

These few words of text brush over the numerous delay-causing problems and setbacks that occur during any construction contract. Simple examples range from local shortages of cement and glass at crucial moments, to sub-contractor delays with a number of key specialist services which cumulatively placed extreme stresses on the schedule. Another significant issue was the lack of available public utilities. In the event, a temporary power source had to be established, as connection with the island's electricity distribution network was delayed until January 2009.

SURGEONS' HALLS

Design features

A number of features of the design, finishes and materials used within the core building and in the campus grounds cleverly illustrate the connectivity or marriage of the cultures of the two islands. The core building is semi-circular in shape, echoing the outward form of Newgrange. Its southern elevation, the view that visitors have from the Shaikh Isa Bin Salman Causeway, is of a structure rising from the ground and then being stepped out at higher levels, loosely reflecting the corbelled ceiling of the burial chamber within the mound at Newgrange (Plate XII, page 66). The colour of the building, a sandy shade of yellow or mustard, settles the whole arrangement comfortably within the landscape yet continues to capture the viewer's interest by its very scale and shape. The vivid white of the tented fabric awning of the atrium, with its scalloped edges, invokes images of desert encampments or the lateen sails of the traditional fishing dhows of the Gulf. On a smaller scale, the fabric styles of the main entrance canopy, the canopy over the gatehouse and the car park shading give similar representations. The external cladding panels contain a cut design which imitates symbols from Newgrange. This pattern is also found on the panels forming the boundary wall on the north side of the campus.

Entering the campus past the gatehouse, visitors notice that the landscaping is contained within areas whose backdrops are retaining stone walls. The stone is local and the style of construction of the walls replicates the dry stone walls that enclose fields throughout Ireland. Again, and mimicking Newgrange, the main traffic roundabout has been built in a grass covered mound formation with dry stone walling (Plate XIII, page 66). The obelisk at the top of ramp to the main entrance, reminiscent of Cleopatra's Needle on the Thames Embankment in London, is inscribed with symbols of megalithic art found inside the burial chamber and on the kerb stones surrounding Newgrange's burial mound (Fig. 2).

On entering the atrium, one is immediately struck by the amount of natural light that is diffused within the space, the cathedral like height of the roof 25 metres above and the colours, fusions and textures of the glass, granite, timber and stone used as final finishes. The height and light create an airy spacious environment. The polished granite floors

[160]

are typical of modern public buildings in the region. What makes this different is the blend of colours; the soft pink Jordanian sandstone, the clear glazed balustrading, the warm honey-coloured timbered panelling, the red brown decorative panels in a Middle Eastern style all crowned by the translucent roof. The Jordanian sandstone wall panels are carved with more representations of megalithic art and the theme is continued with etched whorl shapes on the glass balustrade. In the evenings the chandeliers come into their own as decorative features. The polished chrome finish suggests quality but their shape is what causes real interest. They remind some people of Christmas trees or tree branches, to others they look like coral branches and for some they are reminiscent of arterial systems within the body.

Fig. 2: Images at the base of the obelisk, inspired by Newgrange

Stephen's Green Restaurant

As early as the autumn of 2007, the project control group (Table 3) had recognised that the place where students, staff and visitors would gather to eat would be one of the principal social hubs on the campus and were keen to make it different and yet acceptable to all those who would eventually use the space. All agreed that it should have a distinctive name—Stephen's Green, with its links to the College's homebase, gradually emerged.

In keeping with this, the furniture had to be suitable for a new modern building and also reflect the collegiate nature of the university. The leading light behind this scheme was Spencer Pugh, project manager for Mercury Middle East who had a very clear vision of the Oxbridge style of refectory dining required. The concept was generally supported, but there were doubts about being able to source appropriate tables and seating. Since the Malaysian furniture market was to be the source of the wide range of office furniture and other furnishings, a team was dispatched to the annual furniture fair showing next season's products in Kuala Lumpur in March 2008, with a shopping list for two hectic days of pounding the stands. Late on the first day Spencer Pugh identified a magnificent timber table of some 3 metres in length, 1 metre wide and 12 centimetres deep with the legs being two simple slab off-cuts. The display sample was immense, not only in dimensions, but also in density. The table and other furniture were manufactured in a small village in Sarawak from a sustainable timber called Saur.

The tables were ordered and, being handmade, did not arrive on site until November 2008. Each unit came as a flat pack weighing approximately 250kg. The packs were lifted by crane onto the restaurant's external terrace and then man-handled by eight men into the restaurant for assembly and final positioning. Once they were all in place the impact was exactly as had been hoped (Fig. 3).

Another very visible feature is the wall coverings and prints of Dublin scenes. The contract specification for the wall surfaces and pillars required an emulsion paint finish; however, one of the project team had other ideas. Pearse Cole, project director for Mercury Engineering, had thought that if we could assemble suitable photographs of St Stephen's Green in Dublin and produce wallpaper this would visually establish the identity and theme of the restaurant. Although there were worries over the potential cost of the idea, and the fact that wallpaper was unheard off as a permanent wall finish in the region due to the climate, the imagination of the project team was captured and a photographer, Dominic Lee of Priory Studios in south County Dublin, was commis-

Fig. 3: The Stephen's Green Restaurant

sioned to produce appropriate shots of the Green and its surroundings during the summer of 2008. He visited the Bahrain campus in August and, having seen the wall areas, quickly came up with suggestions for blending various landmarks within the Green such as the duck pond, the fountain and the bandstand. These views offer not only a talking point for visitors, but bring a little bit of St Stephen's Green and Dublin to those studying and working on the campus who may never see the real thing and, for the expatriate, a nice reminder of home.

A spin-off was to print some of the panoramic views on canvas for those walls which would not have wallpaper. The views were shot from the top of a tower crane located at the front of 123 St Stephen's Green. One blend took in the roofs and skyline towards Grafton Street and across the north side of the Green and another looking south over Harcourt Street towards the Dublin Mountains and, now mounted in their current locations in the restaurant, are very effective.

The Frank O'Kane Learning Resource Centre

The Mercury Board, and in particular Frank O'Kane had kept a very close eye on the project's progress and he visited the site frequently. His last visit was in October 2007. Sadly, just before Christmas 2007, Frank was to die suddenly whilst walking in his beloved Wicklow Mountains.

To mark his entrepreneurial leadership, his generosity as an educational benefactor and his close personal involvement with the project, the College asked his family if they would consent to having the Learning Resource Centre named in his memory (Fig. 4). On 3 February 2009 a small informal ceremony of dedication took place in the presence of Frank's family and colleagues. As part of the dedication, a wood engraving of Frank in Spanish chestnut, by artist Larry Ryan of Wicklow, was unveiled.

Fig. 4: The Frank O'Kane Learning Resource Centre

RCSI–MEDICAL UNIVERSITY OF BAHRAIN, 2009

Table 1

Milestones in the development of RCSI–Medical University of Bahrain

October 2003: Memorandum of Understanding signed

2 October 2003: H. H. Shaikh Khalifa Bin Salman Al Khalifa, Prime Minister of the Kingdom of Bahrain conferred with Honorary Fellowship

1 April 2004: First two employees appointed—Mr Riyadh Al Daif and Ms Jo Hinrichson

4 May 2004: Launch of Medical University Bahrain

September 2004: Professor Kevin O'Malley takes up office as President

September 2004: Design for Busaiteen Campus starts

October 2004: Opening of Seef Campus

13 March 2006: Foundation stone laid at Busaiteen Campus

15 March 2006: His Majesty King Hamad Bin Isa Al Khalifa, King of Bahrain, conferred with Honorary Fellowship

15 March 2006: The Order of Bahrain 1st Class awarded to Michael Horgan, CEO RCSI

March–May 2006: Piling phase

15 Dec 2006: Civil and construction contractor on site

Jan 2007: Construction starts

15 August 2008: Contract completion date

11 Sept 2008: First phase partial handover

5 October 2008: Operational opening of the campus

3 February 2009: Formal opening

6 April 2009: Second phase partial handover

1 Sept 2009: Dr Faisil Al Mousawi takes up office as President

24 Nov 2009: Formal opening of Sports Hall

28 June 2010: Inaugural Graduation Ceremony

SURGEONS' HALLS

Table 2

RCSI–Medical University of Bahrain Teaching Space

Existing teaching space	Room no.	Net m²	Seating capacity
Level 01			
Laboratory No 1 (Research Lab)	116	129	40
Laboratory No 2 (Multi-use Lab)	120	120	40
Laboratory No 3 (Clinical Skills Lab)	128	268	25
Lecture Theatre No 1	133	145	165
Lecture Theatre No 2	140	145	165
Level 02			
Laboratory No 4 (Multi-purpose Lab)	219	277	72
Laboratory No 5 (Multi-purpose Lab)	231	248	72
Level 03			
Seminar/Tutorial Room	330	210	100
Level 04			
Group Study Room	419	19	6
Group Study Room	420	22	6
Group Study Room	421	19	7
Group Study Room	422	21	8
Group Study Room	423	21	7
Group Study Room	424	24	12
Group Study Room	425	34	10
Seminar/Tutorial Room	431	79	50
Seminar/Tutorial Room	439	72	50
Seminar/Tutorial Room	440a	38	25–30
Seminar/Tutorial Room	440b	38	25–30
Seminar/Tutorial Room	441a	50	35–40
Seminar/Tutorial Room	441b	50	35–40
Seminar/Tutorial Room	442a	38	25–30
Seminar/Tutorial Room	442b	38	25–30
Seminar/Tutorial Room	445	46	45

RCSI-MEDICAL UNIVERSITY OF BAHRAIN, 2009

Other resources

Level 03

Ladies' Prayer Room	309	23	n/a
Men's Prayer Room	315	34	n/a
Stephen's Green Restaurant	321	484	190
Students' Room	329	49	25
Staff Common Room	326	64	25

Level 04

Frank O'Kane Learning Resource Centre	417	484	84
	435	197	

Sports Building
Ground

Sports Hall	40009	890

First Floor

Male Gym	40108	88
Snooker Room	40116	74
Table Tennis Room	40117	54
Female Gym	40107	85

Table 3

RCSI-Medical University of Bahrain Project Control Group

Professor Kevin O'Malley	President, RCSI-Bahrain
Mrs Mary Alexander	Vice President, Finance & Administration, RCSI-Bahrain
Mr Riyadh Ali Dhaif	Assistant Registrar, RCSI-Bahrain
Ms Jo Hinrichsen	Medical Faculty Administrator, RCSI-Bahrain until April 2008
Mr Colin Stewart	Associate Director Estate & Support Services, RCSI
Mr Jim O'Driscoll	Technical Adviser to RCSI Mott MacDonald Pettit
Mr Pearse Cole	Project Director, Mercury International
Mr Spencer Pugh	Project Manager, Mercury Middle East
Mr Dave Fouhy	Deputy Project Manager, Mercury Middle East until May 2008

[167]

SURGEONS' HALLS

Table 4
RCSI-Medical University of Bahrain Building Data

Fixed price construction cost value (Bahrain Dinars)	19,964,287 (€39,265,325)
Main contractor and project managers	Mercury Middle East
Main civil works	GP Zachariades
Site plot size	96,588 sq m, 9.6 Ha, 24 acres
Core building builtarea	15,758 sq m
No. of spaces within the core building	600
Sports Hall built area	3,093 sq m
Pump room	693 sq m
Service building	825 sq m
Phase I capacity	600+ students & staff
Construction man-hours	1,300,000 hrs
Site manpower at its peak in 2008	800 personnel
No. of piles driven	1,200 no.
Cubic m of concrete	13,500 cu m
5 carrier chillers producing	1,130 kW ea
Water storage underground (pump room area)	920,000 l
No. air handling units	41 no.
No. l lights	5,800 no.
Cable and wire	80 km
Piping	20 km
Max power load consumption	7.5 MW
Weight of copper in low voltage control panels	6 tons